TABLE OF CONTENTS

INTRODUCTION

Welcome to <u>Journaling for Higher Self</u>. The exercises in the Program provide a toolkit that you can use over and over. They are designed to build on one another, beginning with Exercise 1 and continuing through Exercise 6 to get the most benefit. Once you're familiar with the exercises, you can pick and choose which ones call to you at different times for different benefits. I suggest you have extra paper on hand to journal outside the lines provided in this workbook.

NOTE FROM AUTHOR

I have been writing my entire life. Writing to explore, to understand, to process, to be creative. What emerges from my writing is often the unknown, the unexpected, the surprising. And as a result, I often write to find out what I think, how I feel, and how I can develop. I write naturally to feel less emotionally reactive, have more perspective, and to make better choices.

Imagine my sense of validation, when I became a psychotherapist, upon finding decades of studies affirming the therapeutic benefits of writing, suggesting ways I could fold it into my work with clients!

In 2006, I discovered and took my first Internal Family Systems (IFS) training, and through this work, I fell in love with two things I'm hoping this book brings to you now:

- The benefits of working with reactive parts of me.

- Accessing my essential Self—that core we all have that is wise and compassionate, forgiving and kind, resourced and centered, always available in good times and bad.

Of course, developing a writing program at some point to help with that seemed inevitable. The writing program in these pages marries these two modalities, journal writing and Internal Family Systems. It has been through a number of iterations, which means I've used the exercises extensively myself, have had many clients benefit from them, and have offered them in workshops and retreats, including at the IFS Conference in 2017 and as part of my Finding Self in Nature retreat.

I'm thrilled to be offering this program to you in its expanded and updated format. I am confident you will experience the benefits and nutrients of writing to live more fully in your Self energy.

WHY INTERNAL FAMILY SYSTEMS?

Internal Family Systems (IFS) is a transformative psychotherapy model, as well as an empowering paradigm for living life from our best selves. The IFS Institute's website says:

> IFS is a transformative tool that conceives every human being as a system of protective and wounded inner parts lead by a core Self. We believe the mind is naturally multiple and that is a good thing. Just like members of a family, inner parts are forced from their valuable states into extreme roles within us. Self is in everyone. It can't be damaged. It knows how to heal.
> IFS is frequently used as an evidence-based psychotherapy, helping people heal by accessing and healing their protective and wounded inner parts…
>
> IFS is much more than a non-pathologizing evidence-based psychotherapy to be used in a clinical setting. It is also a way of understanding personal and intimate relationships and stepping into life with the 8 Cs: confidence, calm, compassion, courage, creativity, clarity, curiosity, and connectedness.

There are now multiple studies that demonstrate the IFS model is effective in improving mood (depression), increasing the ability to handle chronic pain in a stronger more resourced way, healing trauma, and reducing addiction (internet) symptoms. This program allows you to tap IFS to make changes in your own life and well-being!

WHY JOURNAL WRITING

Expressive writing, like the writing you'll be doing in this program, has been extensively researched over the years (begun in 1986 by James Pennebaker at the University of Texas Austin). The data from myriad studies demonstrate that almost any targeted expressive writing can have therapeutic benefits. Benefits have been significant when writing time is long or short, is on negative emotions or experiences or on positive ones, and personal or not. Participants in studies even benefited from writing about fictional trauma or someone else's difficulties.

The benefits measured in studies endured over time and included such things as improvements in physical health, mood disorders and emotional well-being, life satisfaction, ability to handle stress, better functioning in relationships, moving forward with life choices, and resolving symptoms from trauma. A recent study even suggested that expressive writing helped participants recover from physical injuries more quickly.

Throughout the years dozens of studies have been conducted and best practices have emerged that manifest the best outcomes. These best practices are used in this program so you can experience the maximum benefits of a writing practice!

WHY USE THIS PROGRAM?

This program/workbook is intended to enrich your life in the way adopting a mindfulness meditation practice is intended to enrich your life. Taken as a whole, it is a journaling practice to help you access the resources and strengths you were born with, a practice to help you restore living a life from your powerful essential Self and qualities. In the Internal Family Systems model, these qualities are referred to as Self qualities and when they're present, it's called having Self-energy.

I have found, both in my personal life and working with clients, that we all fall on a continuum of how much Self energy we have access to in our lives and how often. Some of us may have little to none, others have bountiful access. Wherever we fall on that continuum, I believe we would all like more. I know of no better way to access the experience of being in Self, of no better way to develop the capacity to be Self-led in life, than through writing.

When you invest in doing this program and adopting the writing practice, you will be able to live more from Self. Self is the calm, the eye of the storm at our center. Self is the peace that comes with feeling rooted when we take time to settle and feel grounded and centered. Self is the confidence we feel when life is its most challenging yet we know we'll handle whatever we need to. Self is the wisdom of sages that we all have within us, and is the heart-swelling felt sense that comes with being in deep connection with someone or with nature.

IS THIS PROGRAM FOR YOU ?

This program is an excellent choice for anyone working with an IFS therapist, wanting to explore IFS therapy, or get some background on the IFS model as I originally intended. However, like a mindfulness meditation practice, this program can be helpful to most everyone, whether you think of yourself as a writer, someone who journals, or not!

Consider how your life would be different if you had a structured program to help you:

- Be more grounded/centered/emotionally regulated
- Feel more resourced in challenging circumstances
- Easily access your strengths and best qualities and live more in alignment with your best self
- Be less emotionally triggered and have a supportive practice for when you are triggered
- Be less often in fight, flight, freeze responses
- Feel less stressed
- Feel less overwhelmed, stuck, or helpless, and have access to more creative possibilities
- Be more clearheaded
- Gain perspective about and move on from past hurts
- Experience improved physical health and fewer doctor visits
- Move out of feeling conflicted or disempowered
- Find support for and experience fewer insecurities
- Be able to improve relationship dynamics

- Experience more joy, humor, playfulness
- Feel more expansive and have more access to higher meanings and peak experiences
- Get to know your highest Self

WHAT CAN YOU EXPECT

At the end of this program, you can expect to:

~ Know and have a personal experience of each of the 8 qualities of Self— curiosity, compassion, connectedness, confidence, courage, creativity, calm, and clarity
~ Have a toolkit to access those qualities and other Self qualities
~ Have insight into your own internal system and reactions that keep you from staying emotionally regulated
~ Know exercises to support yourself when emotionally triggered or facing challenging times
~ Be able to adopt a consistent writing program for self-care and wellness

HOW TO USE THIS PROGRAM

Research suggests that it takes 6 weeks to adopt new practices or develop new habits, and this program is designed to be completed the first time over the course of 6 weeks. Each week there is a new exercise that builds on the prior weeks and exercises.

You will get the most benefit from doing each exercise multiple times over the week, and the exercises are formatted for you to write 5 days each week. This will allow you to explore the variety of qualities of Self energy and provide you with opportunities to get to know and relate differently to the parts of you that block you from being Self-led. Lastly, it will facilitate you developing the practice of journaling to help you access clarity, wisdom, and creativity, process emotions, make decisions, and/or simply feel well and good.

The exercises are formatted to keep the time spent on each exercise manageable since many of us have busy schedules. Most exercises will require 30–45 minutes minimum, but you can experiment with writing for shorter and longer lengths of time. In Week 5, I provide an example where you can spend as little as 10 minutes writing. If you have more time to spend, that of course allows you to go deeper. However, you don't need to write for long stretches to realize some benefit. The final week is for integration; you will review each of the 5 exercises from the prior weeks.

For each exercise, I provide examples from others who have done the exercise. These examples are to illustrate some possibilities as to what your experience with the exercise might be. However, I encourage you to stay open and curious and allow what shows up for you to be your own. Over and over as I've led these exercises, participants report outcomes that are stunning to them and beautiful to hear. Many report that the experiences and the insights feel deeply connected to their spiritual life and not what they could have predicted.

Once you've completed the program, each exercise works as a stand-alone option. You'll likely find a favorite or favorites you'll go to over and over. I've found that I will have a favorite I use often and then I'll shift to a different one, use it frequently for a time, and so on, circling back to old favorites. My hope for you is that you'll use what I offer here and then get creative and develop some of your own!

WHAT YOU'LL NEED

Something to write in and something to write with. You have space in this book to write, but I always recommend having a side journal/notebook to go longer, and for tangents, which are highly recommended! Some choose to not use the space provided in the book and only journal separately. That can be helpful if it makes writing easier, you want to reuse the book, or it helps you keep your work private.

There is some science to suggest that writing on paper rather than on a digital device is a different experience. Writing on paper engages different brain regions than typing, including the regions involved in long-term memory, emotional experiences, the subconscious, and creativity. Writing on paper also causes us to slow down. These things taken together suggest we may be able to go deeper in our explorations by writing on paper. I recommend you experiment to see what you notice between paper and digital, and between different writing instruments.

A timer. At the beginning of each exercise, I note the range of times the entire exercise will likely take, taking into consideration the time for things like meditations, rereading, and pauses to think. Plan to set aside 30–45 minutes each day. Within each exercise, every prompt has suggested minimum writing times. These suggestions are the absolute shortest amounts of time per prompt to gain optimal benefits. You can always go longer! And you can experiment with writing for a shorter amount of time to notice whether you experience benefits from that. A timer can help you manage time so you complete each exercise in one sitting, which is most ideal.

GUIDELINES TO GET THE MOST OUT OF JOURNALING

Below I offer some general guidelines to get the most out of journaling:

- What you write is personal and private. If you're worried about others finding your journaling, take precautions to keep it private. It is important that you feel safe and free to write what you need to express openly and fully.
- There are no rules to follow in your writing. Don't worry about grammar, punctuation, spelling, the right words, or where you write on the page. Allow for maximum creativity and out-of-the box writing behaviors and thinking. Great pay-off can come from this.
- Ask the part of you who wants to censor what you're saying to take a mini-vacation. What you write may not seem realistic, accurate, reasonable, possible, or right. That is all OK. You don't have to act on anything, or tell anyone anything about what you've written.
- If you don't know what to write in response to a prompt, just start writing. Go with what you write even if it seems like nonsense. Often gems emerge.

- You get to structure how you write to make it most helpful. Although I provide guidelines for each exercise, you can go as long or as short as you want, as deep or as surface-level as feels safe, and write as often as you need to. You get to set your own rules for what's most helpful.
- The exercises are intended to be self-explanatory. If they don't quite make sense, that's okay. Follow the prompts according to what you think is being asked or write based on what makes sense to you.
- Finally, it's recommended that you don't skip the REFLECTION WRITE, which is the last part of every exercise. It changes how you engage with what you've written, brings greater insights, and helps you synthesize and integrate. It provides unexpected and additional benefits.

All the best in your Journaling to Higher Self!

SELF

*There is no cowering energy
in a tree. Nor wavering uncertainty
when the ocean comes to shore.
There are no apologies when dawn
light opens morning's door or
when the sun sets closing it again.
The crocus does not ask permission
to part the earth and break through
winter frost, and nothing of
Nature feels shame.*

WEEK 1 – RECOGNIZING SELF ENERGY
EXERCISE 1 SUGGESTED TIME: 30–45 MINUTES

This first exercise is intended to introduce you to the 8 qualities of Self energy that Dick Schwartz identifies in the Internal Family Systems model. It is designed for you to have a personal experience of each quality so that you have a level of familiarity with the quality rather than just an idea about it. As you're doing this exercise, it's always okay for you to use your imagination to embody any of the qualities if you don't have much personal experience with them.

There are 3 writing prompts for this exercise. The first is a prompt following an introductory meditation to write about one of the C qualities of Self. The second prompt is the REFLECTION WRITE. And the third prompt is to do the meditation and first two prompts over for another C quality.

Each day this week you can repeat the meditation and first 2 prompts for as many of the qualities of Self as you'd like. Over the course of this first week, make sure you write about each of the 8 qualities at least once. You will build on getting to know all of the qualities in upcoming weeks.

EXAMPLE

Jack was in his mid 70s and recently retired from 40 years as a pastor and psychotherapist. He was familiar with the 8 qualities of Self but found himself lacking clarity about what he wanted to do with his next phase of life. This caused him some anxiety and even depression. When doing this first exercise of the program, he first selected Clarity as the quality he wanted more of.

Jack's feedback following the exercise was that he strongly connected with a memory of being a young camp counselor leading a group of teens on a backpacking weekend in the mountains. One evening during the weekend, there was an unexpected storm that scattered the group and one of the teens didn't return to the base camp. Throughout that evening and the next morning, Jack had clarity about how to handle the situation and support the group even though he knew the situation could turn into a crisis. Ultimately, they suspended the search for the evening when it got dark and resumed in the morning, following Jack's plan for the search. They found the teen shaken but no worse for wear.

For Jack, the exercise allowed him to connect physically with the clarity he had, and as a result, he was able to fully access that resource again. By being in that resourced state, he was able to consider different possibilities and had less anxiety. As he did the exercise subsequent times and spent time in the different Self qualities, he crafted a vision for what he wanted the next phase of his life to include and had clarity about how to make it happen.

You can no doubt hear many of the other Self qualities that were present for Jack alongside clarity, such as confidence, courage, and calm. This is common.

INSTRUCTIONS

WEEK 1 Day 1: Choose one of the 8 C qualities of Self that you'd like to explore or have more of in your life:

Curiosity

Connection

Compassion

Courage

Confidence

Calm

Creativity

Clarity

MEDITATION

Get comfortable, let your eyes soften or close, and take a few deep breaths in and out.

When you're settled, allow yourself to remember a time in your life when you had the quality you've chosen. If you don't remember having the quality, let yourself imagine what it might be like to have that quality. Just notice what you can. Take some time to remember or imagine what accompanies having this quality:

       the Physical Felt Sense,
              pause
       the Feelings,
              pause
       the Thinking and Thoughts,
              pause
       the Behaviors,
              pause

WEEK 1 Day 1

When you're ready, write about the experience of having this quality.

Recommended minimum write time: 3 minutes.
Optimal write time: 5–7 minutes

_____

_____

_____

_____

_____

_____

_____

_____

_____

_____

_____

_____

_____

_____

_____

_____

_____

REFLECTION WRITE

Re-read what you've journaled and write a reflection on the process of writing about this quality, any insights/awarenesses that came from journaling, or anything else you noticed.

Recommended minimum write time: 3 minutes.

_____

_____

_____

_____

_____

_____

_____

_____

_____

_____

_____

_____

_____

_____

_____

_____

_____

OPTIONAL

Repeat the exercise to experience several or all of the C qualities of Self. Add the quality of Acceptance or any other quality you associate with being in Self energy to write about.

_____

_____

_____

_____

_____

_____

_____

_____

_____

_____

_____

_____

_____

_____

_____

_____

_____

_____

INSTRUCTIONS

WEEK 1 Day 2: Choose one of the 8 C qualities of Self that you'd like to explore or have more of in your life:

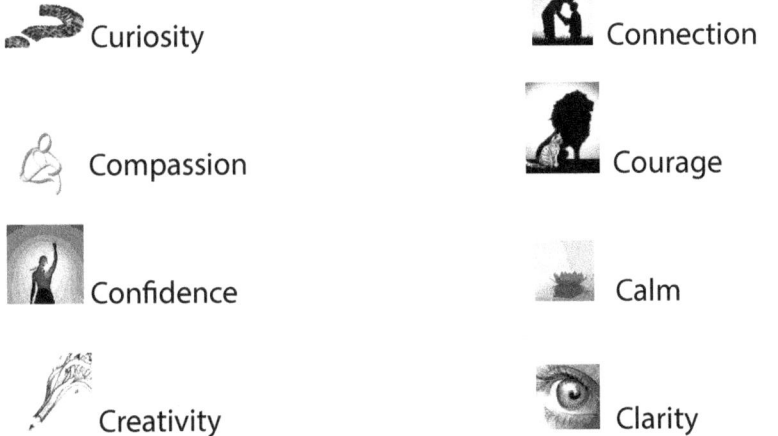

Curiosity

Connection

Compassion

Courage

Confidence

Calm

Creativity

Clarity

MEDITATION

Get comfortable, let your eyes soften or close, and take a few deep breaths in and out.

When you're settled, allow yourself to remember a time in your life when you had the quality you've chosen. If you don't remember having the quality, let yourself imagine what it might be like to have that quality. Just notice what you can. Take some time to remember or imagine what accompanies having this quality:

> the Physical Felt Sense,
> > pause
> the Feelings,
> > pause
> the Thinking and Thoughts,
> > pause
> the Behaviors,
> > pause

When you're ready, write about the experience of having this quality.

Recommended minimum write time: 3 minutes.
Optimal write time: 5–7 minutes

_____

_____

_____

_____

_____

_____

_____

_____

_____

_____

_____

_____

_____

_____

_____

_____

_____

REFLECTION WRITE

Re-read what you've journaled and write a reflection on the process of writing about this quality, any insights/awarenesses that came from journaling, or anything else you noticed.

Recommended minimum write time: 3 minutes.

_____

_____

_____

_____

_____

_____

_____

_____

_____

_____

_____

_____

_____

_____

_____

_____

_____

OPTIONAL

Repeat the exercise to experience several or all of the C qualities of Self. Add the quality of Acceptance or any other quality you associate with being in Self energy to write about.

_____

_____

_____

_____

_____

_____

_____

_____

_____

_____

_____

_____

_____

_____

_____

INSTRUCTIONS

WEEK 1 Day 3: Choose one of the 8 C qualities of Self that you'd like to explore or have more of in your life:

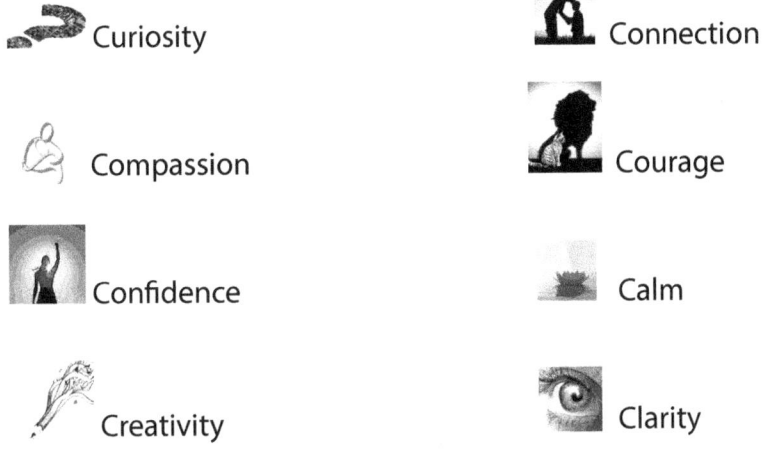

Curiosity   Connection

Compassion   Courage

Confidence   Calm

Creativity   Clarity

MEDITATION

Get comfortable, let your eyes soften or close, and take a few deep breaths in and out.

When you're settled, allow yourself to remember a time in your life when you had the quality you've chosen. If you don't remember having the quality, let yourself imagine what it might be like to have that quality. Just notice what you can. Take some time to remember or imagine what accompanies having this quality:

> the Physical Felt Sense,
> > pause
> the Feelings,
> > pause
> the Thinking and Thoughts,
> > pause
> the Behaviors,
> > pause

When you're ready, write about the experience of having this quality.

WEEK 1 Day 3:

Recommended minimum write time: 3 minutes.
Optimal write time: 5–7 minutes

_____

_____

_____

_____

_____

_____

_____

_____

_____

_____

_____

_____

_____

_____

_____

_____

_____

_____

REFLECTION WRITE

Re-read what you've journaled and write a reflection on the process of writing about this quality, any insights/awarenesses that came from journaling, or anything else you noticed.

Recommended minimum write time: 3 minutes.

_____

_____

_____

_____

_____

_____

_____

_____

_____

_____

_____

_____

_____

_____

_____

OPTIONAL

Repeat the exercise to experience several or all of the C qualities of Self. Add the quality of Acceptance or any other quality you associate with being in Self energy to write about.

_____

_____

_____

_____

_____

_____

_____

_____

_____

_____

_____

_____

_____

_____

_____

_____

_____

INSTRUCTIONS

WEEK 1 Day 4: Choose one of the 8 C qualities of Self that you'd like to explore or have more of in your life:

Curiosity

Connection

Compassion

Courage

Confidence

Calm

Creativity

Clarity

MEDITATION

Get comfortable, let your eyes soften or close, and take a few deep breaths in and out.

When you're settled, allow yourself to remember a time in your life when you had the quality you've chosen. If you don't remember having the quality, let yourself imagine what it might be like to have that quality. Just notice what you can. Take some time to remember or imagine what accompanies having this quality:

the Physical Felt Sense,
pause
the Feelings,
pause
the Thinking and Thoughts,
pause
the Behaviors,
pause

When you're ready, write about the experience of having this quality.

Recommended minimum write time: 3 minutes.
Optimal write time: 5–7 minutes

_____

_____

_____

_____

_____

_____

_____

_____

_____

_____

_____

_____

_____

_____

_____

_____

_____

REFLECTION WRITE

Re-read what you've journaled and write a reflection on the process of writing about this quality, any insights/awarenesses that came from journaling, or anything else you noticed.

Recommended minimum write time: 3 minutes.

_____

_____

_____

_____

_____

_____

_____

_____

_____

_____

_____

_____

_____

_____

_____

_____

_____

_____

OPTIONAL

Repeat the exercise to experience several or all of the C qualities of Self. Add the quality of Acceptance or any other quality you associate with being in Self energy to write about.

_____

_____

_____

_____

_____

_____

_____

_____

_____

_____

_____

_____

_____

_____

_____

_____

_____

INSTRUCTIONS

WEEK 1 Day 5: Choose one of the 8 C qualities of Self that you'd like to explore or have more of in your life:

Curiosity   Connection

Compassion   Courage

Confidence   Calm

Creativity   Clarity

MEDITATION

Get comfortable, let your eyes soften or close, and take a few deep breaths in and out.

When you're settled, allow yourself to remember a time in your life when you had the quality you've chosen. If you don't remember having the quality, let yourself imagine what it might be like to have that quality. Just notice what you can. Take some time to remember or imagine what accompanies having this quality:

> the Physical Felt Sense,
>> pause
> the Feelings,
>> pause
> the Thinking and Thoughts,
>> pause
> the Behaviors,
>> pause

When you're ready, write about the experience of having this quality.

Recommended minimum write time: 3 minutes.
Optimal write time: 5–7 minutes

_____

_____

_____

_____

_____

_____

_____

_____

_____

_____

_____

_____

_____

_____

_____

_____

_____

_____

REFLECTION WRITE

Re-read what you've journaled and write a reflection on the process of writing about this quality, any insights/awarenesses that came from journaling, or anything else you noticed.

Recommended minimum write time: 3 minutes.

_____

_____

_____

_____

_____

_____

_____

_____

_____

_____

_____

_____

_____

_____

_____

_____

OPTIONAL

 Repeat the exercise to experience several or all of the C qualities of Self. Add the quality of Acceptance or any other quality you associate with being in Self energy to write about.

_____

_____

_____

_____

_____

_____

_____

_____

_____

_____

_____

_____

_____

_____

_____

_____

_____

MY INSECURITY PART

She buzzes within me today,
insecurity animated, while I try
to write. My mind wanders to
the rose bush outside captured
by the first bloom of pink, a richer
shade than I remember under
the steely gray cloud cover. But
insecurity is the pin of fear that sticks
me to this notepad, wings stilled, an object,
and I'm unable to fly.

WEEK 2 – EXPANDING SELF ENERGY

EXERCISE 2 - SUGGESTED TIME: 30–45 MINUTES

Part of the genius of the IFS model is in recognizing that Parts of us can be in the lead in ways that block us from leading with our Self energy and best qualities. This is called Parts being blended with us. Because of our histories, these Parts can have extreme protective responses or behaviors to people or situations, can hold difficult emotions, and can hold unhelpful beliefs or expectations. They can even show up physically as sensations or reactions in our bodies. When we get to know and listen to these Parts who are unhelpful because of the ways they've become extreme, they unblend so we have more access to Self qualities and energy.

The intention for this exercise is to introduce you to how Parts of us can be in the lead and to create experiences of shifting to Self being in the lead instead. It builds on what we did last week where we became familiar with each of the 8 C qualities of Self. It is intended to help you experience Parts unblending and increase access to more Self energy.

There are 3 writing prompts for this exercise. The first is a prompt to get to know a Part of you. That is followed by a prompt to write to the Part from one, several, or all of the C qualities of Self. You can choose how many you write from, but I recommend that at least one of the days this week you write a response from all qualities; it's a powerful way to be with Parts and can dramatically change how we relate to them and how they show up. The third prompt is the **REFLECTION WRITE**.

For this exercise, each day of the week you can choose a different Part of you or you can continue with only one Part throughout the week.

EXAMPLE

Catherine was in her 40s and preparing for a knee repair surgery when she did this exercise. She had a part of her with extreme anxiety about the surgery and recovery so she wasn't able to sleep nights or focus to get through her work day, even though she was assured it wasn't a threatening procedure. She wrote about this Part and realized that its fear came from stories about her grandfather dying young during a heart surgery.

The first Self quality she responded to this part from was Compassion. Recognizing and being with the Part by writing from Compassion resulted in its anxiety quieting. It is often the case that Parts quiet just from being met with compassion. Writing from other C qualities allowed the Part to be even less blended with her so she could access her Courage and Confidence. Leading up to the surgery, she was then able to sleep better and be more available for her work, and was also able to really receive and feel the support of her family. She reported being more optimistic, calm, and confident.

INSTRUCTIONS

WEEK 2 DAY 1: Choose a Part of yourself that you'd like to understand better, know more about, or work with. A Part may show up as a reaction, behavior, physical condition, body sensation, or strong feeling. When it's time to write about the Part, you have options:

- You can write in your own voice about this Part,
- You can allow this Part to write what it wants to say, or
- You can write for this Part saying what it has said to or shown you.
- I encourage you to experiment with writing from these different perspectives throughout the week.

MEDITATION

Get comfortable, let your eyes soften or close, and take a few deep breaths in and out.

When you're settled, bring your awareness to the Part of you you've chosen. Let yourself get curious about this Part and how it shows up:

> the Physical Felt Sense or Energy of it,
> > *pause*
> Its Feelings,
> > *pause*
> Its Thinking and Thoughts,
> > *pause*
> Its Behaviors,
> > *pause*

When you're ready, write about what you noticed. You have options about how to write:

- You can write in your own voice about this Part,
- You can allow this Part to write what it wants to say, or
- You can write for this Part saying what it has said or shown you.

Recommended minimum write time: 5–10 minutes.

WEEK 2 DAY 1:

_____

_____

_____

_____

_____

_____

_____

_____

_____

_____

_____

_____

_____

_____

_____

_____

_____

_____

_____

INSTRUCTIONS

Re-read what you've written.

Now bring your awareness to the 8 C qualities we explored last week in Exercise 1. If it's helpful, you can do the Exercise 1 Meditation here to reconnect with any of those qualities. When you're ready, write a response to the Part you're spending time with from one, some, or all of the 8 C qualities of Self, and from Acceptance.

Recommended minimum write time: 3–5 minutes per quality

Write a response from **Curiosity**

_____

_____

_____

_____

_____

_____

_____

_____

_____

_____

_____

Write a response from **Compassion**

_____

_____

_____

_____

_____

_____

_____

_____

_____

Write a response from **Connection**

_____

_____

_____

_____

_____

_____

_____

_____

_____

Write a response from **Calm**

_____

_____

_____

_____

_____

_____

_____

_____

_____

Write a response from **Courage**

_____

_____

_____

_____

_____

_____

_____

_____

_____

Write a response from **Creativity**

_____

_____

_____

_____

_____

_____

_____

_____

Write a response from **Confidence**

_____

_____

_____

_____

_____

_____

_____

_____

_____

Write a response from **Clarity**

_____

_____

_____

_____

_____

_____

_____

_____

_____

Write a response from **Acceptance**

_____

_____

_____

_____

_____

_____

_____

_____

_____

REFLECTION WRITE

Re-read what you've journaled and write a reflection on the process of writing from these qualities, any insights/awarenesses that came from journaling, or anything else you noticed.

Recommended minimum write time: 3 minutes

INSTRUCTIONS

WEEK 2 DAY 2: Choose a Part of yourself that you'd like to understand better, know more about, or work with. A Part may show up as a reaction, behavior, physical condition, body sensation, or strong feeling. When it's time to write about the Part, you have options:

- You can write in your own voice about this Part,
- You can allow this Part to write what it wants to say, or
- You can write for this Part saying what it has said to or shown you.
- I encourage you to experiment with writing from these different perspectives throughout the week.

MEDITATION

Get comfortable, let your eyes soften or close, and take a few deep breaths in and out.

When you're settled, bring your awareness to the Part of you you've chosen. Let yourself get curious about this Part and how it shows up:

the Physical Felt Sense or Energy of it,
> *pause*

Its Feelings,
> *pause*

Its Thinking and Thoughts,
> *pause*

Its Behaviors,
> *pause*

When you're ready, write about what you noticed. You have options about how to write:

- You can write in your own voice about this Part,
- You can allow this Part to write what it wants to say, or
- You can write for this Part saying what it has said or shown you.

Recommended minimum write time: 5–10 minutes.

WEEK 2 DAY 2:

_____

_____

_____

_____

_____

_____

_____

_____

_____

_____

_____

_____

_____

_____

_____

_____

_____

_____

_____

_____

INSTRUCTIONS

Re-read what you've written.

Now bring your awareness to the 8 C qualities we explored last week in Exercise 1. If it's helpful, you can do the Exercise 1 Meditation here to reconnect with any of those qualities. When you're ready, write a response to the Part you're spending time with from one, some, or all of the 8 C qualities of Self, and from Acceptance.

Recommended minimum write time: 3–5 minutes per quality

Write a response from **Curiosity**

_____

_____

_____

_____

_____

_____

_____

_____

_____

_____

_____

Write a response from 👤 **Compassion**

_____

_____

_____

_____

_____

_____

_____

_____

_____

Write a response from 👥 **Connection**

_____

_____

_____

_____

_____

_____

_____

_____

_____

_____

Write a response from **Calm**

_____

_____

_____

_____

_____

_____

_____

_____

_____

Write a response from **Courage**

_____

_____

_____

_____

_____

_____

_____

_____

_____

Write a response from **Creativity**

_____

_____

_____

_____

_____

_____

_____

_____

_____

Write a response from **Confidence**

_____

_____

_____

_____

_____

_____

_____

_____

_____

Write a response from **Clarity**

_____

_____

_____

_____

_____

_____

_____

_____

_____

Write a response from **Acceptance**

_____

_____

_____

_____

_____

_____

_____

_____

_____

WEEK 2 DAY 2:

REFLECTION WRITE

Re-read what you've journaled and write a reflection on the process of writing from these qualities, any insights/awarenesses that came from journaling, or anything else you noticed.

Recommended minimum write time: 3 minutes

_____

_____

_____

_____

_____

_____

_____

_____

_____

_____

_____

_____

_____

_____

INSTRUCTIONS

WEEK 2 DAY 3: Choose a Part of yourself that you'd like to understand better, know more about, or work with. A Part may show up as a reaction, behavior, physical condition, body sensation, or strong feeling. When it's time to write about the Part, you have options:

- You can write in your own voice about this Part,
- You can allow this Part to write what it wants to say, or
- You can write for this Part saying what it has said to or shown you.
- I encourage you to experiment with writing from these different perspectives throughout the week.

MEDITATION

Get comfortable, let your eyes soften or close, and take a few deep breaths in and out.

When you're settled, bring your awareness to the Part of you you've chosen. Let yourself get curious about this Part and how it shows up:

> the Physical Felt Sense or Energy of it,
> > *pause*
> Its Feelings,
> > *pause*
> Its Thinking and Thoughts,
> > *pause*
> Its Behaviors,
> > *pause*

When you're ready, write about what you noticed. You have options about how to write:

- You can write in your own voice about this Part,
- You can allow this Part to write what it wants to say, or
- You can write for this Part saying what it has said or shown you.

Recommended minimum write time: 5–10 minutes.

WEEK 2 DAY 3:

_____

_____

_____

_____

_____

_____

_____

_____

_____

_____

_____

_____

_____

_____

_____

_____

_____

_____

_____

_____

_____

_____

INSTRUCTIONS

Re-read what you've written.

Now bring your awareness to the 8 C qualities we explored last week in Exercise 1. If it's helpful, you can do the Exercise 1 Meditation here to reconnect with any of those qualities. When you're ready, write a response to the Part you're spending time with from one, some, or all of the 8 C qualities of Self, and from Acceptance.

Recommended minimum write time: 3–5 minutes per quality

Write a response from **Curiosity**

_____

_____

_____

_____

_____

_____

_____

_____

_____

_____

Write a response from **Compassion**

_____

_____

_____

_____

_____

_____

_____

_____

Write a response from **Connection**

_____

_____

_____

_____

_____

_____

_____

_____

_____

Write a response from **Calm**

_____

_____

_____

_____

_____

_____

_____

_____

_____

Write a response from **Courage**

_____

_____

_____

_____

_____

_____

_____

_____

_____

Write a response from **Creativity**

_____

_____

_____

_____

_____

_____

_____

_____

Write a response from **Confidence**

_____

_____

_____

_____

_____

_____

_____

_____

_____

Write a response from **Clarity**

_____

_____

_____

_____

_____

_____

_____

_____

_____

Write a response from **Acceptance**

_____

_____

_____

_____

_____

_____

_____

_____

_____

REFLECTION WRITE

Re-read what you've journaled and write a reflection on the process of writing from these qualities, any insights/awarenesses that came from journaling, or anything else you noticed.

Recommended minimum write time: 3 minutes

_____

_____

_____

_____

_____

_____

_____

_____

_____

_____

_____

_____

_____

_____

_____

INSTRUCTIONS

WEEK 2 DAY 4: Choose a Part of yourself that you'd like to understand better, know more about, or work with. A Part may show up as a reaction, behavior, physical condition, body sensation, or strong feeling. When it's time to write about the Part, you have options:

- You can write in your own voice about this Part,
- You can allow this Part to write what it wants to say, or
- You can write for this Part saying what it has said to or shown you.
- I encourage you to experiment with writing from these different perspectives throughout the week.

MEDITATION

Get comfortable, let your eyes soften or close, and take a few deep breaths in and out.

When you're settled, bring your awareness to the Part of you you've chosen. Let yourself get curious about this Part and how it shows up:

> the Physical Felt Sense or Energy of it,
> > *pause*
> Its Feelings,
> > *pause*
> Its Thinking and Thoughts,
> > *pause*
> Its Behaviors,
> > *pause*

When you're ready, write about what you noticed. You have options about how to write:

- You can write in your own voice about this Part,
- You can allow this Part to write what it wants to say, or
- You can write for this Part saying what it has said or shown you.

Recommended minimum write time: 5–10 minutes.

_____

_____

_____

_____

_____

_____

_____

_____

_____

_____

_____

_____

_____

_____

_____

_____

_____

_____

_____

_____

INSTRUCTIONS

Re-read what you've written.

Now bring your awareness to the 8 C qualities we explored last week in Exercise 1. If it's helpful, you can do the Exercise 1 Meditation here to reconnect with any of those qualities. When you're ready, write a response to the Part you're spending time with from one, some, or all of the 8 C qualities of Self, and from Acceptance.

Recommended minimum write time: 3–5 minutes per quality

Write a response from **Curiosity**

_____

_____

_____

_____

_____

_____

_____

_____

_____

_____

Write a response from **Compassion**

_____

_____

_____

_____

_____

_____

_____

_____

Write a response from **Connection**

_____

_____

_____

_____

_____

_____

_____

_____

Write a response from **Calm**

_____

_____

_____

_____

_____

_____

_____

_____

_____

Write a response from **Courage**

_____

_____

_____

_____

_____

_____

_____

_____

_____

Write a response from **Creativity**

_____

_____

_____

_____

_____

_____

_____

_____

Write a response from **Confidence**

_____

_____

_____

_____

_____

_____

_____

_____

_____

Write a response from **Clarity**

_____

_____

_____

_____

_____

_____

_____

_____

_____

Write a response from **Acceptance**

_____

_____

_____

_____

_____

_____

_____

_____

_____

REFLECTION WRITE

Re-read what you've journaled and write a reflection on the process of writing from these qualities, any insights/awarenesses that came from journaling, or anything else you noticed.

Recommended minimum write time: 3 minutes

_____

_____

_____

_____

_____

_____

_____

_____

_____

_____

_____

_____

_____

_____

_____

INSTRUCTIONS

WEEK 2 DAY 5: Choose a Part of yourself that you'd like to understand better, know more about, or work with. A Part may show up as a reaction, behavior, physical condition, body sensation, or strong feeling. When it's time to write about the Part, you have options:

- You can write in your own voice about this Part,
- You can allow this Part to write what it wants to say, or
- You can write for this Part saying what it has said to or shown you.
- I encourage you to experiment with writing from these different perspectives throughout the week.

MEDITATION

Get comfortable, let your eyes soften or close, and take a few deep breaths in and out.

When you're settled, bring your awareness to the Part of you you've chosen. Let yourself get curious about this Part and how it shows up:

> the Physical Felt Sense or Energy of it,
> > *pause*
> Its Feelings,
> > *pause*
> Its Thinking and Thoughts,
> > *pause*
> Its Behaviors,
> > *pause*

When you're ready, write about what you noticed. You have options about how to write:

- You can write in your own voice about this Part,
- You can allow this Part to write what it wants to say, or
- You can write for this Part saying what it has said or shown you.

Recommended minimum write time: 5–10 minutes.

INSTRUCTIONS

Re-read what you've written.

Now bring your awareness to the 8 C qualities we explored last week in Exercise 1. If it's helpful, you can do the Exercise 1 Meditation here to reconnect with any of those qualities. When you're ready, write a response to the Part you're spending time with from one, some, or all of the 8 C qualities of Self, and from Acceptance.

Recommended minimum write time: 3–5 minutes per quality

Write a response from **Curiosity**

_____

_____

_____

_____

_____

_____

_____

_____

_____

_____

WEEK 2 DAY 5:

Write a response from **Compassion**

_____

_____

_____

_____

_____

_____

_____

_____

_____

Write a response from **Connection**

_____

_____

_____

_____

_____

_____

_____

_____

_____

_____

_____

Write a response from **Calm**

_____

_____

_____

_____

_____

_____

_____

_____

_____

Write a response from **Courage**

_____

_____

_____

_____

_____

_____

_____

_____

_____

Write a response from **Creativity**

_____

_____

_____

_____

_____

_____

_____

_____

Write a response from **Confidence**

_____

_____

_____

_____

_____

_____

_____

_____

_____

Write a response from **Clarity**

_____

_____

_____

_____

_____

_____

_____

_____

_____

Write a response from **Acceptance**

_____

_____

_____

_____

_____

_____

_____

_____

_____

WEEK 2 DAY 5:

REFLECTION WRITE

Re-read what you've journaled and write a reflection on the process of writing from these qualities, any insights/awarenesses that came from journaling, or anything else you noticed.

Recommended minimum write time: 3 minutes

_____

_____

_____

_____

_____

_____

_____

_____

_____

_____

_____

_____

_____

_____

LIKE WATER

We are like water.
We take the shape of whatever vessel
we are in, though we remain our selves
even as we are shaped by what
holds us. If I mistake
the shape from my
life for my
essence, I will
miss what
slakes my
thirst.

WEEK 3 – BRINGING SELF ENERGY TO A CLUSTER OF PARTS

EXERCISE 3

SUGGESTED TIME: 30–45 MINUTES

Exercise 3 utilizes a technique you might be familiar with called the cluster-write. It is a way to brainstorm and visually organize related information. For us, it will be a way to identify multiple Parts of us related to an issue, problem, concern, or behavior. Writing in this visual way can help access unconscious material, reveal connections, and provide a visual of the psychic energy involved in what you're exploring.

There are a lot of intentions for this exercise! First, it provides an understanding of how your Parts are all participants in your internal system—the system at the center of the Internal Family Systems model. Just like the families we grew up in, internally we have Parts who are close and connected with one another and Parts who can be at odds or split off.

The exercise is also designed to give you a visual representation. This visual map about different issues you struggle with can help immensely with gaining understanding and new perspectives. Having a visual picture can be worth a thousand words!

And most importantly, the exercise provides opportunities for you to understand your system from Self qualities and experience how that can transform how you relate to your system as a whole. Relating from this mindful perspective minimizes how disorganizing it can feel when jumping around amongst different perspectives and reactions. It helps you notice when you have different Parts in the lead so you can be more Self-led rather than Parts-led.

There are 4 writing prompts for this exercise. The first is a prompt to create your cluster using the template provided. The second is a prompt to identify the Parts that are part of the cluster and show the connections and polarizations between Parts. The third prompt is to write about the cluster from one, several, or all of the C qualities of Self. And lastly, the final prompt is the **REFLECTION WRITE**.

EXAMPLE

Janet did this exercise in her late 30s as she was considering going back to work because her 3 children were all in school. She was very conflicted and feeling a lot of anxiety around this choice, so that's what she put in her center box. She chose a feeling she was struggling with, but she could have named it "Going Back to Work." Attached are illustrations of how she completed the template for the first prompt and then for the second prompt where she noted Parts and whether they were aligned or polarized.

The first Self quality she wrote about bringing to her cluster was Courage. This helped her perspective shift from the younger parts of her who felt small and not capable of knowing she can handle difficult challenges. The next quality that she wrote from was Confidence because that showed up naturally as she wrote from Courage. By writing from these 2 qualities, she was able to notice when young fearful Parts blended with her, so she next chose to write from Calm. She was then feeling much more Clarity, which she reinforced by writing from that quality. With her anxiety greatly reduced and having more clarity, she was able to make the choice that felt honoring of all her Parts—to return to work at a job where she trusted she could balance working and being a parent.

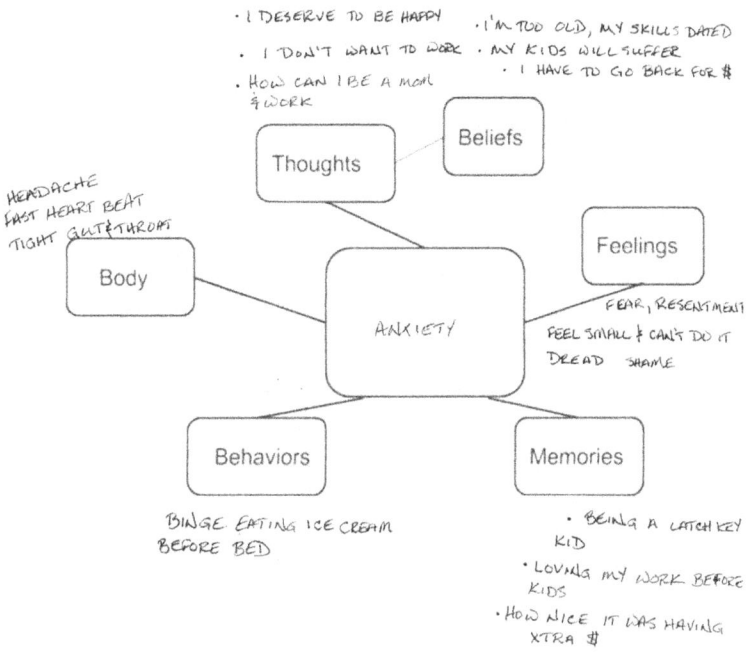

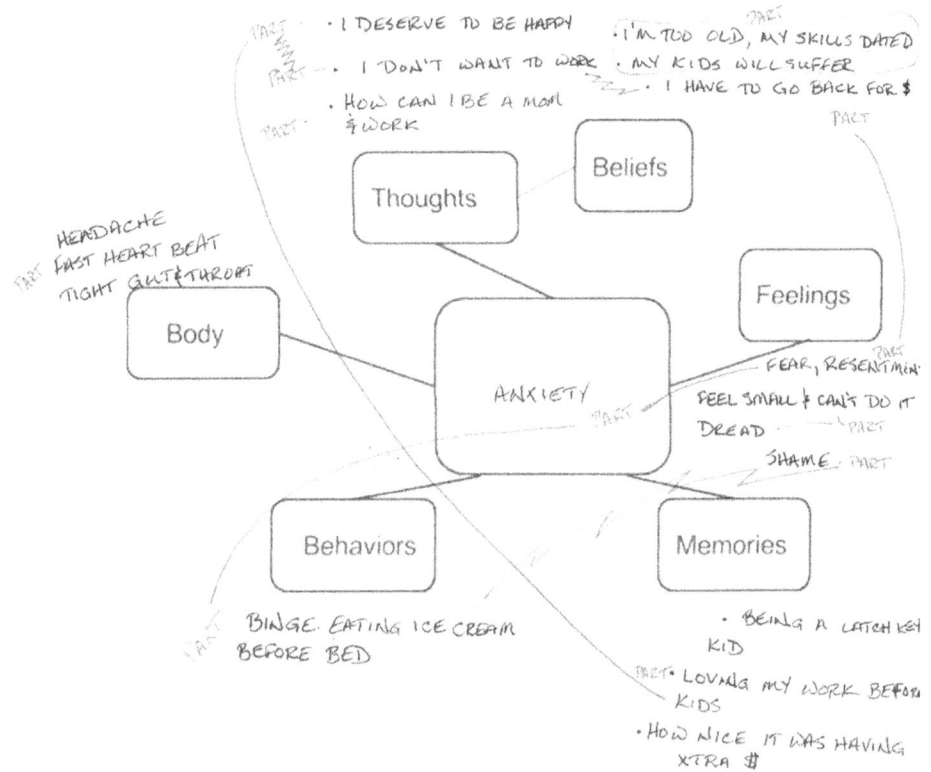

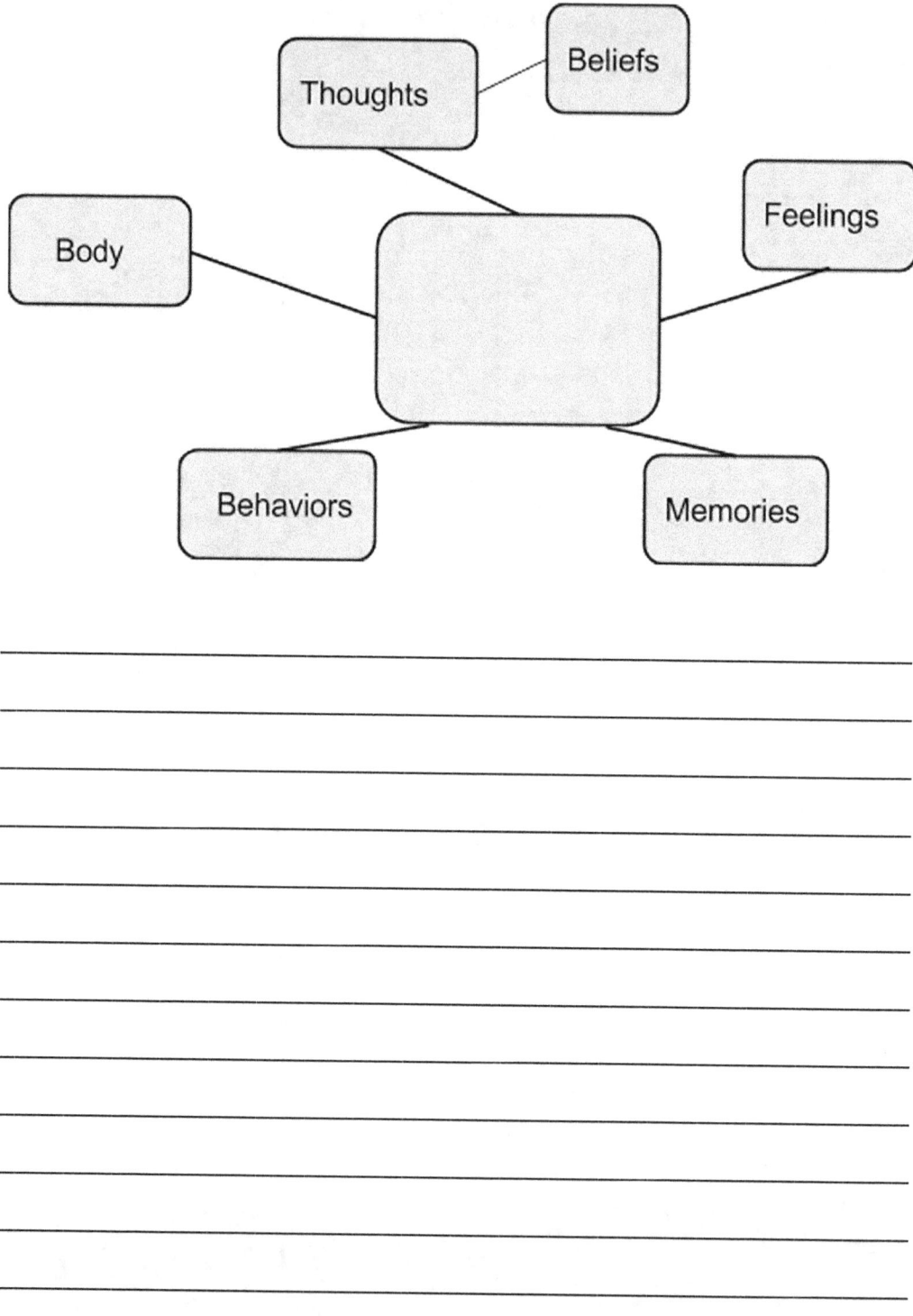

_____

_____

_____

_____

_____

_____

_____

_____

_____

_____

_____

_____

INSTRUCTIONS

WEEK 3 Day 1: Take a few moments to think about and select a personal issue, problem, concern, or behavior that you'd like to understand more about.

Name what you've selected in the center circle of the Cluster Write template provided.

For each of the labeled boxes on the template, write 1–3 quick associations next to the box. Write as quickly as possible without judging or censoring what comes to mind. This helps you to access subconscious material.

Recommended minimum write time: 5–7 minutes

Take a couple of moments to review your cluster. Notice within the cluster anything that feels like a Part of you and circle or label it. Typically, you'll see a number of Parts associated with the cluster. For example, if you started with Depression (one of your Parts) as your issue to explore (in the center box), you may find an Expectation Part who has a general fear and expectation of getting in trouble, a Behavior Part who acts out by drinking because of that fear, and a Memory Part who holds the memory of always being in trouble with your parents.

If you'd like to go the next step, you can use a solid line to connect Parts of you that are aligned and a squiggly line to connect Parts of you that are at odds. For instance, in the example above, there's the Feeling Part who drinks to manage fear and there might be a Feeling Part who has shame about that. These would be connected with a squiggly line. The Part with the expectation of getting in trouble would be connected with a solid line to the Part who drinks. Don't worry if your sheet gets messy.

Recommended minimum write time: 5 minutes

Now bring your awareness to the 8 C qualities we explored in Week 1 Exercise 1. If it's helpful, you can do the Exercise 1 Meditation here to reconnect with any of those qualities.

Choose one of the 8 C qualities of Self, the quality of Acceptance, or one of your own choosing. Write for a couple of minutes about what it is like or would be like to bring that quality to this cluster of Parts.

Then select another Self quality and write for a couple of minutes about what it is like or would be like to bring that quality to this cluster. Allow time so that you can explore a couple or all of the qualities below.

Recommended minimum write time: 5 minutes per quality

Curiosity

Courage

Compassion

Calm

Confidence

Clarity

Creativity

Acceptance

Connection

Write a response from _____

_____

_____

_____

_____

_____

_____

_____

_____

_____

Write a response from _____

_____

_____

_____

_____

_____

_____

_____

_____

_____

Write a response from _____

_____

_____

_____

_____

_____

_____

_____

_____

_____

REFLECTION WRITE

Re-read what you've journaled and write a reflection on the process of doing the cluster, identifying Parts, and writing from Self qualities, including any insights/ awarenesses that came from journaling, or anything else you noticed.

Recommended minimum write time: 3 minutes

_____

_____

_____

_____

_____

_____

_____

_____

_____

_____

_____

_____

_____

_____

_____

_____

_____

INSTRUCTIONS

WEEK 3 Day 2: Take a few moments to think about and select a personal issue, problem, concern, or behavior that you'd like to understand more about.

Name what you've selected in the center circle of the Cluster Write template provided.

For each of the labeled boxes on the template, write 1–3 quick associations next to the box. Write as quickly as possible without judging or censoring what comes to mind. This helps you to access subconscious material.

Recommended minimum write time: 5–7 minutes

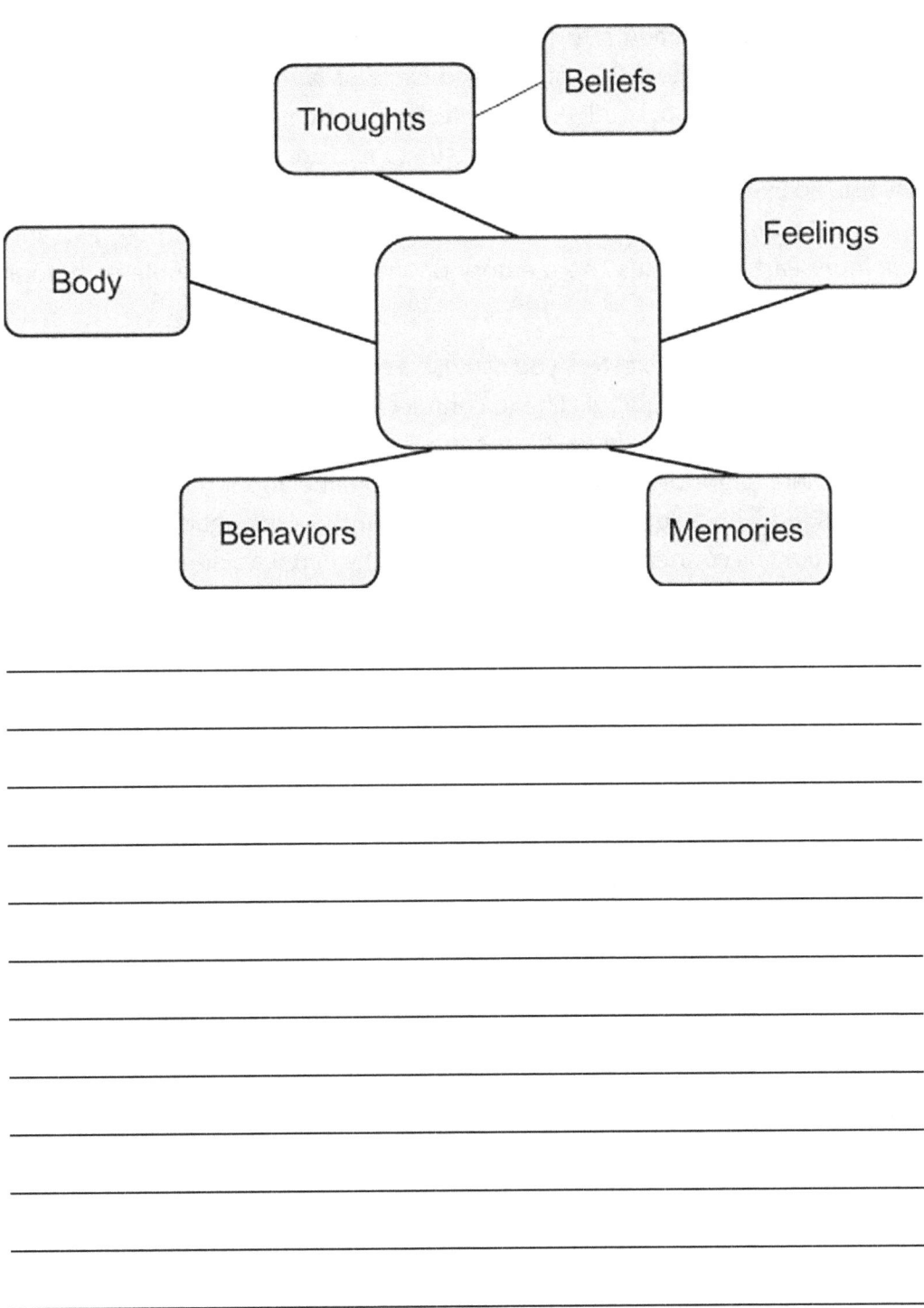

_____

_____

_____

_____

_____

_____

_____

_____

_____

_____

_____

_____

Take a couple of moments to review your cluster. Notice within the cluster anything that feels like a Part of you and circle or label it. Typically, you'll see a number of Parts associated with the cluster. For example, if you started with Depression (one of your Parts) as your issue to explore (in the center box), you may find an Expectation Part who has a general fear and expectation of getting in trouble, a Behavior Part who acts out by drinking because of that fear, and a Memory Part who holds the memory of always being in trouble with your parents.

If you'd like to go the next step, you can use a solid line to connect Parts of you that are aligned and a squiggly line to connect Parts of you that are at odds. For instance, in the example above, there's the Feeling Part who drinks to manage fear and there might be a Feeling Part who has shame about that. These would be connected with a squiggly line. The Part with the expectation of getting in trouble would be connected with a solid line to the Part who drinks. Don't worry if your sheet gets messy.

Recommended minimum write time: 5 minutes

Now bring your awareness to the 8 C qualities we explored in Week 1 Exercise 1. If it's helpful, you can do the Exercise 1 Meditation here to reconnect with any of those qualities.

Choose one of the 8 C qualities of Self, the quality of Acceptance, or one of your own choosing. Write for a couple of minutes about what it is like or would be like to bring that quality to this cluster of Parts.

Then select another Self quality and write for a couple of minutes about what it is like or would be like to bring that quality to this cluster. Allow time so that you can explore a couple or all of the qualities below.

Recommended minimum write time: 5 minutes per quality

Curiosity

Courage

Compassion

Calm

Confidence

Clarity

Creativity

Acceptance

Connection

Write a response from _____

_____

_____

_____

_____

_____

_____

_____

_____

_____

_____

Write a response from _____

_____

_____

_____

_____

_____

_____

_____

_____

_____

Write a response from _____

_____

_____

_____

_____

_____

_____

_____

_____

_____

REFLECTION WRITE

Re-read what you've journaled and write a reflection on the process of doing the cluster, identifying Parts, and writing from Self qualities, including any insights/ awarenesses that came from journaling, or anything else you noticed.

Recommended minimum write time: 3 minutes

_____

_____

_____

_____

_____

_____

_____

_____

_____

_____

_____

_____

_____

_____

_____

_____

_____

INSTRUCTIONS

WEEK 3 Day 3: Take a few moments to think about and select a personal issue, problem, concern, or behavior that you'd like to understand more about.

Name what you've selected in the center circle of the Cluster Write template provided.

For each of the labeled boxes on the template, write 1–3 quick associations next to the box. Write as quickly as possible without judging or censoring what comes to mind. This helps you to access subconscious material.

Recommended minimum write time: 5–7 minutes

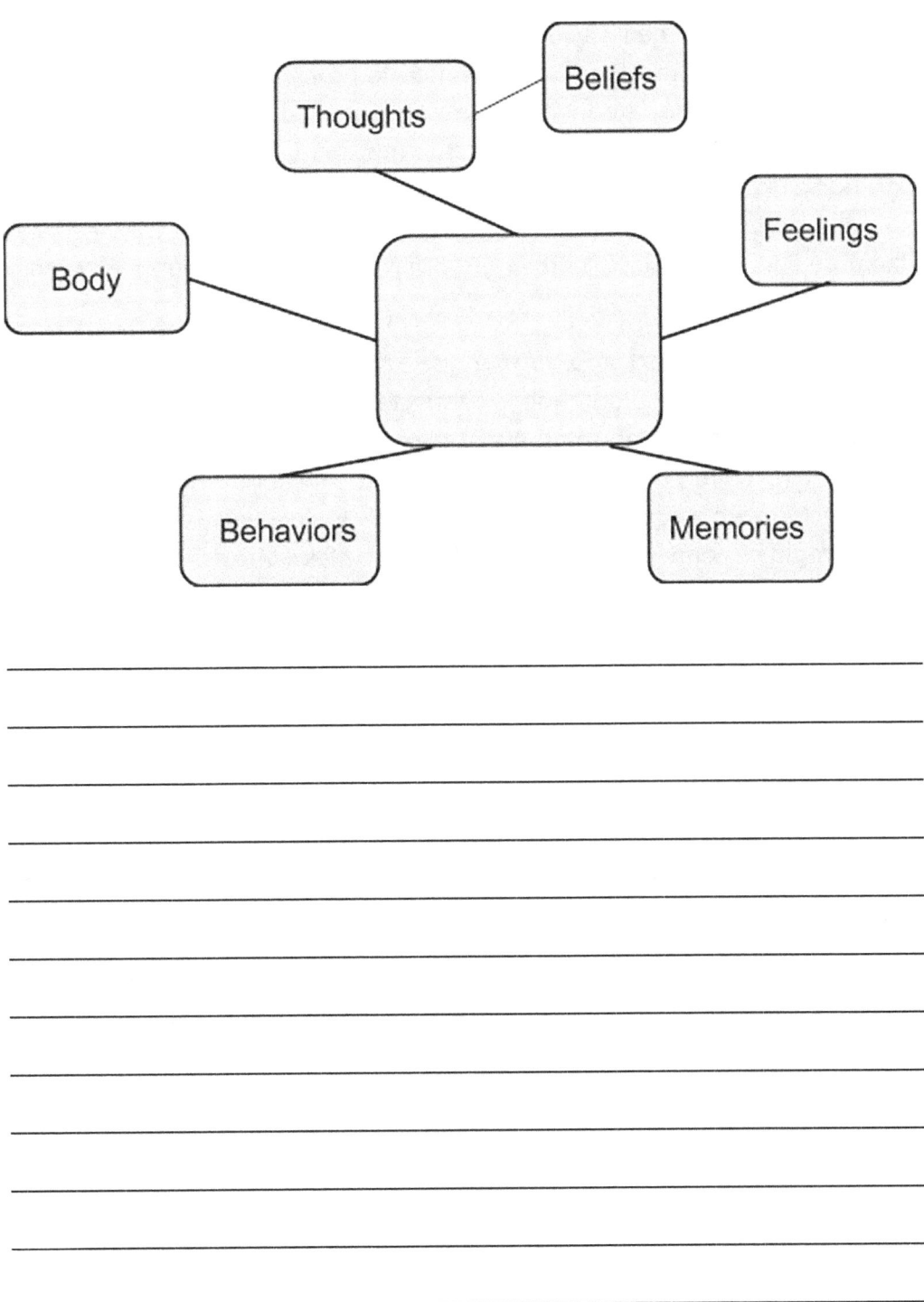

_____

_____

_____

_____

_____

_____

_____

_____

_____

_____

_____

_____

Take a couple of moments to review your cluster. Notice within the cluster anything that feels like a Part of you and circle or label it. Typically, you'll see a number of Parts associated with the cluster. For example, if you started with Depression (one of your Parts) as your issue to explore (in the center box), you may find an Expectation Part who has a general fear and expectation of getting in trouble, a Behavior Part who acts out by drinking because of that fear, and a Memory Part who holds the memory of always being in trouble with your parents.

If you'd like to go the next step, you can use a solid line to connect Parts of you that are aligned and a squiggly line to connect Parts of you that are at odds. For instance, in the example above, there's the Feeling Part who drinks to manage fear and there might be a Feeling Part who has shame about that. These would be connected with a squiggly line. The Part with the expectation of getting in trouble would be connected with a solid line to the Part who drinks. Don't worry if your sheet gets messy.

Recommended minimum write time: 5 minutes

Now bring your awareness to the 8 C qualities we explored in Week 1 Exercise 1. If it's helpful, you can do the Exercise 1 Meditation here to reconnect with any of those qualities.

Choose one of the 8 C qualities of Self, the quality of Acceptance, or one of your own choosing. Write for a couple of minutes about what it is like or would be like to bring that quality to this cluster of Parts.

Then select another Self quality and write for a couple of minutes about what it is like or would be like to bring that quality to this cluster. Allow time so that you can explore a couple or all of the qualities below.

Recommended minimum write time: 5 minutes per quality

Curiosity

Courage

Compassion

Calm

Confidence

Clarity

Creativity

Acceptance

Connection

Write a response from _____

_____

_____

_____

_____

_____

_____

_____

_____

_____

_____

Write a response from _____

_____

_____

_____

_____

_____

_____

_____

_____

Write a response from _____

_____

_____

_____

_____

_____

_____

_____

_____

_____

REFLECTION WRITE

Re-read what you've journaled and write a reflection on the process of doing the cluster, identifying Parts, and writing from Self qualities, including any insights/ awarenesses that came from journaling, or anything else you noticed.

Recommended minimum write time: 3 minutes

_____

_____

_____

_____

_____

_____

_____

_____

_____

_____

_____

_____

_____

_____

_____

_____

INSTRUCTIONS

WEEK 3 Day 4: Take a few moments to think about and select a personal issue, problem, concern, or behavior that you'd like to understand more about.

Name what you've selected in the center circle of the Cluster Write template provided.

For each of the labeled boxes on the template, write 1–3 quick associations next to the box. Write as quickly as possible without judging or censoring what comes to mind. This helps you to access subconscious material.

Recommended minimum write time: 5–7 minutes

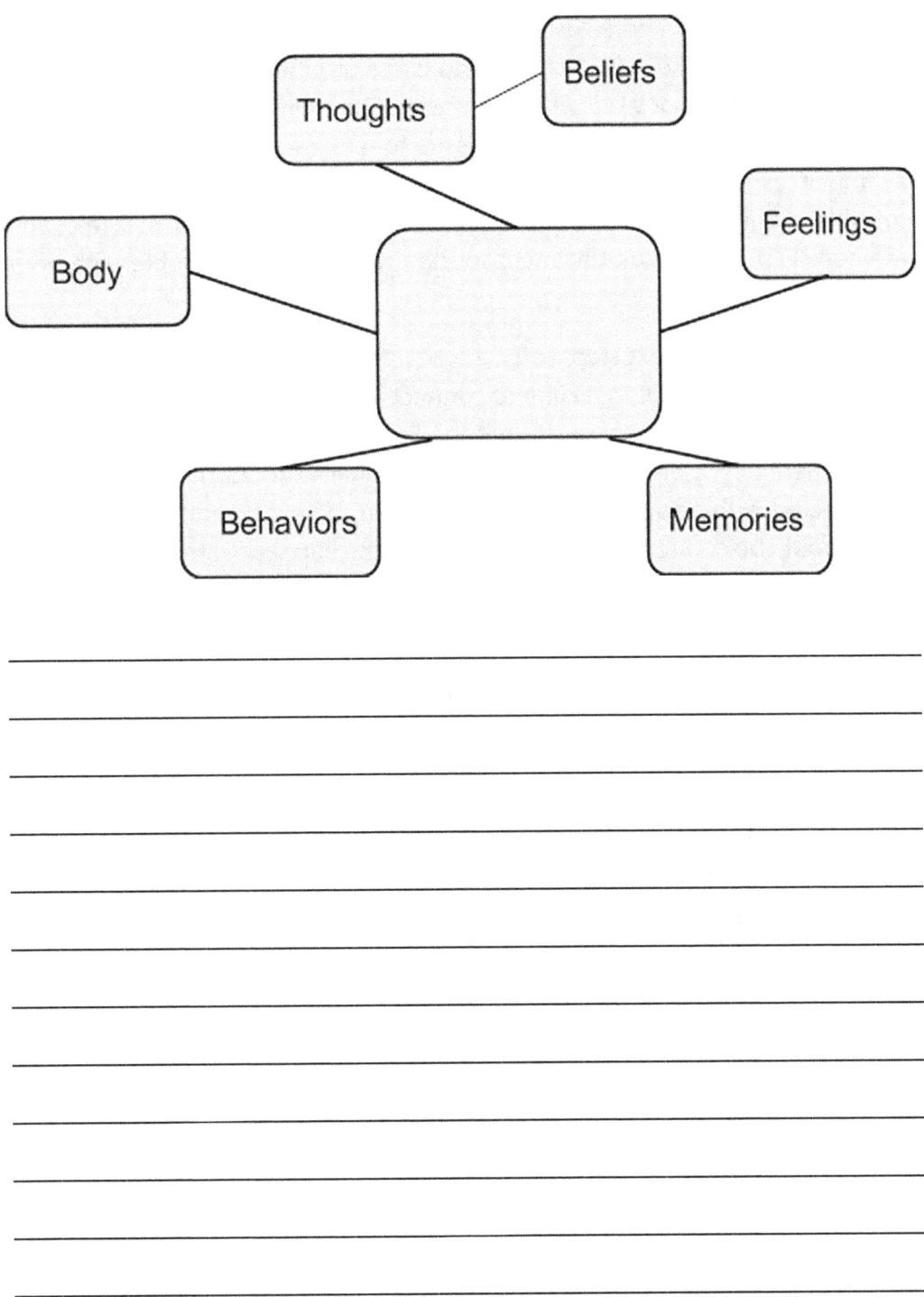

_____

_____

_____

_____

_____

_____

_____

_____

_____

_____

_____

Take a couple of moments to review your cluster. Notice within the cluster anything that feels like a Part of you and circle or label it. Typically, you'll see a number of Parts associated with the cluster. For example, if you started with Depression (one of your Parts) as your issue to explore (in the center box), you may find an Expectation Part who has a general fear and expectation of getting in trouble, a Behavior Part who acts out by drinking because of that fear, and a Memory Part who holds the memory of always being in trouble with your parents.

If you'd like to go the next step, you can use a solid line to connect Parts of you that are aligned and a squiggly line to connect Parts of you that are at odds. For instance, in the example above, there's the Feeling Part who drinks to manage fear and there might be a Feeling Part who has shame about that. These would be connected with a squiggly line. The Part with the expectation of getting in trouble would be connected with a solid line to the Part who drinks. Don't worry if your sheet gets messy.

Recommended minimum write time: 5 minutes

Now bring your awareness to the 8 C qualities we explored in Week 1 Exercise 1. If it's helpful, you can do the Exercise 1 Meditation here to reconnect with any of those qualities.

Choose one of the 8 C qualities of Self, the quality of Acceptance, or one of your own choosing. Write for a couple of minutes about what it is like or would be like to bring that quality to this cluster of Parts.

Then select another Self quality and write for a couple of minutes about what it is like or would be like to bring that quality to this cluster. Allow time so that you can explore a couple or all of the qualities below.

Recommended minimum write time: 5 minutes per quality

Curiosity

Courage

Compassion

Calm

Confidence

Clarity

Creativity

Acceptance

Connection

Write a response from _____

_____

_____

_____

_____

_____

_____

_____

_____

_____

_____

Write a response from _____

_____

_____

_____

_____

_____

_____

_____

_____

Write a response from _____

_____

_____

_____

_____

_____

_____

_____

_____

_____

_____

REFLECTION WRITE

Re-read what you've journaled and write a reflection on the process of doing the cluster, identifying Parts, and writing from Self qualities, including any insights/awarenesses that came from journaling, or anything else you noticed.

Recommended minimum write time: 3 minutes

_____

_____

_____

_____

_____

_____

_____

_____

_____

_____

_____

_____

_____

_____

_____

INSTRUCTIONS

WEEK 3 Day 5: Take a few moments to think about and select a personal issue, problem, concern, or behavior that you'd like to understand more about.

Name what you've selected in the center circle of the Cluster Write template provided.

For each of the labeled boxes on the template, write 1–3 quick associations next to the box. Write as quickly as possible without judging or censoring what comes to mind. This helps you to access subconscious material.

Recommended minimum write time: 5–7 minutes

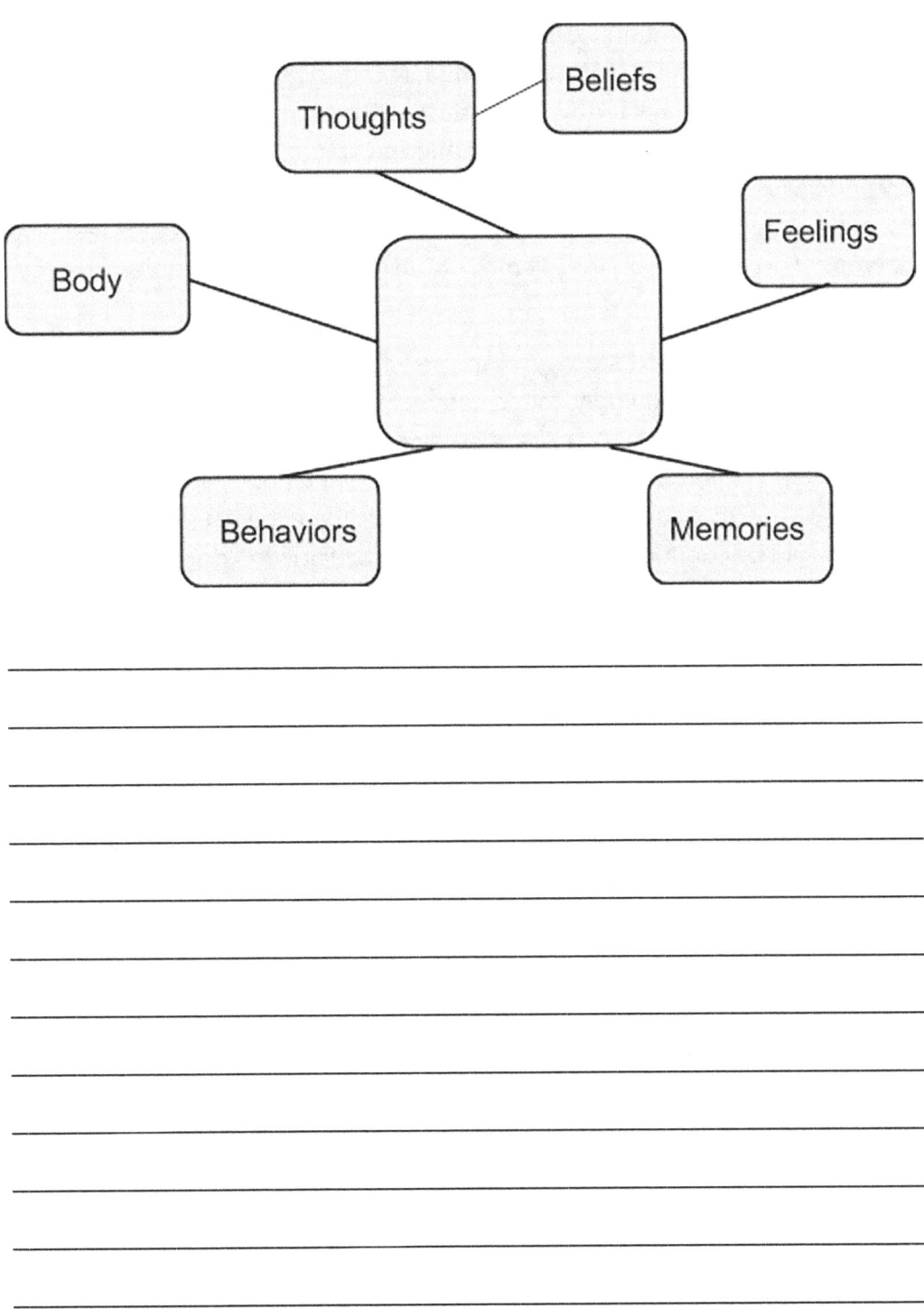

_____
_____
_____
_____
_____
_____
_____
_____
_____
_____
_____

Take a couple of moments to review your cluster. Notice within the cluster anything that feels like a Part of you and circle or label it. Typically, you'll see a number of Parts associated with the cluster. For example, if you started with Depression (one of your Parts) as your issue to explore (in the center box), you may find an Expectation Part who has a general fear and expectation of getting in trouble, a Behavior Part who acts out by drinking because of that fear, and a Memory Part who holds the memory of always being in trouble with your parents.

If you'd like to go the next step, you can use a solid line to connect Parts of you that are aligned and a squiggly line to connect Parts of you that are at odds. For instance, in the example above, there's the Feeling Part who drinks to manage fear and there might be a Feeling Part who has shame about that. These would be connected with a squiggly line. The Part with the expectation of getting in trouble would be connected with a solid line to the Part who drinks. Don't worry if your sheet gets messy.

Recommended minimum write time: 5 minutes

Now bring your awareness to the 8 C qualities we explored in Week 1 Exercise 1. If it's helpful, you can do the Exercise 1 Meditation here to reconnect with any of those qualities.

Choose one of the 8 C qualities of Self, the quality of Acceptance, or one of your own choosing. Write for a couple of minutes about what it is like or would be like to bring that quality to this cluster of Parts.

Then select another Self quality and write for a couple of minutes about what it is like or would be like to bring that quality to this cluster. Allow time so that you can explore a couple or all of the qualities below.

Recommended minimum write time: 5 minutes per quality

Curiosity

Courage

Compassion

Calm

Confidence

Clarity

Creativity

Acceptance

Connection

Write a response from _____

_____

_____

_____

_____

_____

_____

_____

_____

_____

Write a response from _____

_____

_____

_____

_____

_____

_____

_____

_____

_____

Write a response from _____

_____

_____

_____

_____

_____

_____

_____

_____

_____

REFLECTION WRITE

Re-read what you've journaled and write a reflection on the process of doing the cluster, identifying Parts, and writing from Self qualities, including any insights/awarenesses that came from journaling, or anything else you noticed.

Recommended minimum write time: 3 minutes

_____

_____

_____

_____

_____

_____

_____

_____

_____

_____

_____

_____

_____

_____

_____

_____

_____

MY BEING

Disapproval glares down on me
from nowhere but the long distant
memory of your harsh opinion,
of your inability to see me, and
unwillingness to support.
My being configured around
your disapproval so I can't
make a different choice to be
different, despite the deep
protests echoing within,
protests who won't be silenced,
protests doggedly insistent on
me reclaiming, reconfiguring, restoring.
Insistent that I take the uncleared path
and learn to live under a different gaze,
the gaze of appreciation and approval.

WEEK 4 – BRINGING SELF TO RELATIONSHIP TRIGGERS

EXERCISE 4

SUGGESTED TIME: 30–45 MINUTES

Relationships may be the primary area of our lives where we lose our ability to be Self-led—to stay grounded, centered, emotionally regulated, and show up as our best selves. At times we may not even be clear about why Parts of us react in such an extreme way. Even when we do have some understanding, unless we address what I like to call the subtext of why we're triggered, we often can't make different choices to respond differently. Our reflexive responses to the subtext are too powerful.

This exercise is intended to help you identify some of the subtexts in relationships that can be so triggering to Parts of you. An example of subtext might be the interpretation that when your partner is controlling it's because they believe they're better than you and their message is you're not capable of doing what they're controlling over.

As with the other exercises in this program, this exercise is for you to experience being with your triggered Parts from Self qualities, and experience them unblending and you shifting into more Self energy.

Also, this exercise is intended to help you find that it doesn't matter if the subtext belief/message is true for you to benefit from having more Self energy. In the example above, your partner may not actually believe they're better than you. When you have clarity and calm about that, your reactive Parts understand they don't need to respond.

However, your partner may have a Part of them who actually believes they're better than you. Being more Self-led means you can respond with more creativity and clarity and calm rather than from your reactive Parts. In both cases, you are less reactive and stay more emotionally regulated even though nothing has changed with your partner!

There are 3 writing prompts for this exercise. The first will be a prompt to invite the Part you find during the meditation to write whatever it wants to say. That is followed by a prompt to write to the Part from one, several, or all of the C qualities of Self. Lastly, the third prompt is the REFLECTION WRITE.

This exercise has many permutations that can be done throughout the week. For example:

> Each day you do this exercise, you can do the prompts for one Part. Or

> Do the prompts for multiple Parts. For example, during the meditation, you may find a Part with anxiety is the first that shows up. Once you've completed the prompts for that Part, you can do the meditation for the same trigger again. You may find a Part with anger, or another emotion, and you can complete all the prompts for that Part, and so on.

> On each of the 5 writing days for this exercise, you can return to the same relationship trigger and do the prompts for one or multiple Parts. Or

You can start with a new relationship trigger each day, and do the prompts for one or multiple Parts.

If that all sounds too confusing, don't worry about doing the exercise for more than one triggered Part each day. I include the paragraph above for consideration only for those who will want to do more.

EXAMPLE

Bethany had been with her partner Matt for 20 years and loved him deeply. However, in all those years, she consistently considered leaving him because "he didn't make her a priority." As much as she tried to coach him on what he could do—plan date nights, choose to spend time with her over time with old friends he didn't care about who came to town, do something special when she had something good or extra difficult happen in her life—it seemed like he was incapable of getting it.

As she did this exercise, the core belief she thought Matt held about her was that she didn't matter and he could take her for granted because she'd never leave. The first Part of her that she noticed was one who was angry and frustrated. This response was very familiar to her and was where her thoughts about leaving him came from. What this Part wanted to scream at Matt (and did when it wrote) was that she didn't deserve how he treated her, that she deserved to be prioritized and treated as special, and that she will leave him! When she wrote to this Part from Compassion, then Curiosity, then Connection, she realized it was young and angry from having a mother who was always too busy with work to spend time with her. With that understanding, the anger quieted.

When she did the meditation again, the next Part she noticed was a Part who held the hurt from not feeling like she mattered to her mother or to Matt. When this Part wrote, it wanted to tell Matt about how deep the hurt was and how alone and neglected it felt. Bethany wrote responses to this Part from Compassion, Connection, and Clarity. Afterwards, she shared that her Part felt less sad and alone, and she had clarity that Matt wasn't perfect but that she did matter to him and he did prioritize her in ways she hadn't been able to see.

WEEK 4 Day 1:

MEDITATION

Get comfortable, let your eyes soften or close, and take a few deep breaths in and out.

Once you're settled, take some moments to choose someone who triggers a Part/reaction/response in you that you'd like to explore, understand better, or work with.

As you picture this person, notice what it's like to be with them, how you feel, what you think, and how your body responds.

Now ask yourself, what do I imagine is this person's core belief about me or their core message to me? Write down what you believe their core beliefs/messages are.

Once you've identified what you imagine is their core belief or message, scan your body and find the first reaction/response/feeling you notice; you can notice this as how one Part of you reacts. Invite the Part to write below what it wants to say to or about the person who triggers you.

Recommended minimum write time: 3–5 minutes

_____

_____

_____

_____

_____

_____

_____

_____

_____

_____

_____

_____

_____

_____

_____

_____

_____

_____

_____

_____

_____

_____

_____

_____

_____

_____

_____

_____

INSTRUCTIONS

Re-read what the Part of you journaled. Now bring your awareness to the 8 C qualities we explored in Week 1 Exercise 1. If it's helpful, you can do the Exercise 1 Meditation here to reconnect with any of those qualities. Choose one of the qualities and write a response to the Part from that quality. Repeat this step so that you write a response from several of the qualities below.

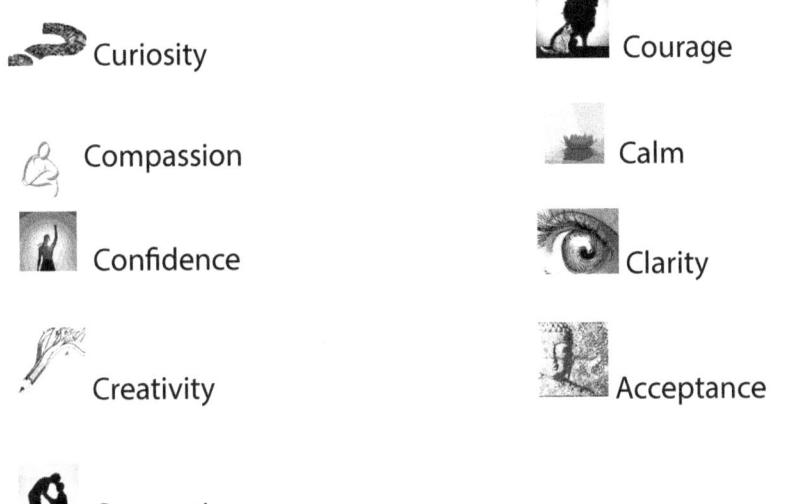

Curiosity

Courage

Compassion

Calm

Confidence

Clarity

Creativity

Acceptance

Connection

Recommended minimum write time: 3–5 minutes per quality

Write a response from _____

_____

_____

_____

_____

_____

_____

_____

_____

_____

Write a response from _____

_____

_____

_____

_____

_____

_____

_____

_____

_____

Write a response from _____

_____

_____

_____

_____

_____

_____

_____

_____

_____

_____

OPTIONAL

Repeat the above sequence, starting again with the Meditation until all reacting parts have written and received feedback from Self qualities.

_____

_____

_____

_____

_____

_____

_____

_____

_____

_____

_____

_____

_____

_____

_____

_____

REFLECTION WRITE

Re-read what you've journaled and write a reflection on the process of writing, any insights/awarenesses that came from journaling, or anything else you noticed.

Recommended minimum write time: 3 minutes

_____

_____

_____

_____

_____

_____

_____

_____

_____

_____

_____

_____

_____

_____

_____

_____

_____

_____

WEEK 4 Day 2:

MEDITATION

Get comfortable, let your eyes soften or close, and take a few deep breaths in and out.

Once you're settled, take some moments to choose someone who triggers a Part/reaction/response in you that you'd like to explore, understand better, or work with.

As you picture this person, notice what it's like to be with them, how you feel, what you think, and how your body responds.

Now ask yourself, what do I imagine is this person's core belief about me or their core message to me? Write down what you believe their core beliefs/messages are.

Once you've identified what you imagine is their core belief or message, scan your body and find the first reaction/response/feeling you notice; you can notice this as how one Part of you reacts. Invite the Part to write below what it wants to say to or about the person who triggers you.

Recommended minimum write time: 3–5 minutes

_____

_____

_____

_____

_____

_____

_____

INSTRUCTIONS

Re-read what the Part of you journaled. Now bring your awareness to the 8 C qualities we explored in Week 1 Exercise 1. If it's helpful, you can do the Exercise 1 Meditation here to reconnect with any of those qualities. Choose one of the qualities and write a response to the Part from that quality. Repeat this step so that you write a response from several of the qualities below.

Curiosity

Courage

Compassion

Calm

Confidence

Clarity

Creativity

Acceptance

Connection

Recommended minimum write time: 3–5 minutes per quality

Write a response from _____

_____

_____

_____

_____

_____

_____

_____

_____

_____

Write a response from _____

_____

_____

_____

_____

_____

_____

_____

_____

_____

Write a response from _____

_____

_____

_____

_____

_____

_____

_____

_____

_____

_____

OPTIONAL

Repeat the above sequence, starting again with the Meditation until all reacting parts have written and received feedback from Self qualities.

_____

_____

_____

_____

_____

_____

_____

_____

_____

_____

_____

_____

_____

_____

_____

_____

_____

_____

_____

REFLECTION WRITE

Re-read what you've journaled and write a reflection on the process of writing, any insights/awarenesses that came from journaling, or anything else you noticed.

Recommended minimum write time: 3 minutes

_____

_____

_____

_____

_____

_____

_____

_____

_____

_____

_____

_____

_____

_____

_____

_____

_____

WEEK 4 Day 3:

MEDITATION

Get comfortable, let your eyes soften or close, and take a few deep breaths in and out.

Once you're settled, take some moments to choose someone who triggers a Part/reaction/response in you that you'd like to explore, understand better, or work with.

 As you picture this person, notice what it's like to be with them, how you feel, what you think, and how your body responds.

Now ask yourself, what do I imagine is this person's core belief about me or their core message to me? Write down what you believe their core beliefs/messages are.

Once you've identified what you imagine is their core belief or message, scan your body and find the first reaction/response/feeling you notice; you can notice this as how one Part of you reacts. Invite the Part to write below what it wants to say to or about the person who triggers you.

Recommended minimum write time: 3–5 minutes

_____

_____

_____

_____

_____

_____

_____

_____

_____

_____

_____

_____

_____

_____

_____

_____

_____

_____

_____

_____

_____

_____

_____

_____

_____

_____

_____

_____

_____

_____

INSTRUCTIONS

Re-read what the Part of you journaled. Now bring your awareness to the 8 C qualities we explored in Week 1 Exercise 1. If it's helpful, you can do the Exercise 1 Meditation here to reconnect with any of those qualities. Choose one of the qualities and write a response to the Part from that quality. Repeat this step so that you write a response from several of the qualities below.

Curiosity

Courage

Compassion

Calm

Confidence

Clarity

Creativity

Acceptance

Connection

Recommended minimum write time: 3–5 minutes per quality

Write a response from _____

_____

_____

_____

_____

_____

_____

_____

_____

_____

Write a response from _____

_____

_____

_____

_____

_____

_____

_____

_____

_____

Write a response from _____

_____

_____

_____

_____

_____

_____

_____

_____

_____

_____

OPTIONAL

Repeat the above sequence, starting again with the Meditation until all reacting parts have written and received feedback from Self qualities.

_____

_____

_____

_____

_____

_____

_____

_____

_____

_____

_____

_____

_____

_____

_____

_____

_____

REFLECTION WRITE

Re-read what you've journaled and write a reflection on the process of writing, any insights/awarenesses that came from journaling, or anything else you noticed.

Recommended minimum write time: 3 minutes

_____

_____

_____

_____

_____

_____

_____

_____

_____

_____

_____

_____

_____

_____

_____

_____

_____

_____

WEEK 4 Day 4:

MEDITATION

Get comfortable, let your eyes soften or close, and take a few deep breaths in and out.

Once you're settled, take some moments to choose someone who triggers a Part/reaction/response in you that you'd like to explore, understand better, or work with.

As you picture this person, notice what it's like to be with them, how you feel, what you think, and how your body responds.

Now ask yourself, what do I imagine is this person's core belief about me or their core message to me? Write down what you believe their core beliefs/messages are.

Once you've identified what you imagine is their core belief or message, scan your body and find the first reaction/response/feeling you notice; you can notice this as how one Part of you reacts. Invite the Part to write below what it wants to say to or about the person who triggers you.

Recommended minimum write time: 3–5 minutes

_____

_____

_____

_____

_____

_____

_____

_____

INSTRUCTIONS

Re-read what the Part of you journaled. Now bring your awareness to the 8 C qualities we explored in Week 1 Exercise 1. If it's helpful, you can do the Exercise 1 Meditation here to reconnect with any of those qualities. Choose one of the qualities and write a response to the Part from that quality. Repeat this step so that you write a response from several of the qualities below.

Curiosity

Courage

Compassion

Calm

Confidence

Clarity

Creativity

Acceptance

Connection

Recommended minimum write time: 3–5 minutes per quality

Write a response from _____

_____

_____

_____

_____

_____

_____

_____

_____

_____

Write a response from _____

_____

_____

_____

_____

_____

_____

_____

_____

_____

Write a response from _____

_____

_____

_____

_____

_____

_____

_____

_____

_____

OPTIONAL

Repeat the above sequence, starting again with the Meditation until all reacting parts have written and received feedback from Self qualities.

_____

_____

_____

_____

_____

_____

_____

_____

_____

_____

_____

_____

_____

_____

_____

_____

_____

_____

REFLECTION WRITE

Re-read what you've journaled and write a reflection on the process of writing, any insights/awarenesses that came from journaling, or anything else you noticed.

Recommended minimum write time: 3 minutes

_____

_____

_____

_____

_____

_____

_____

_____

_____

_____

_____

_____

_____

_____

_____

_____

_____

WEEK 4 Day 5:

MEDITATION

Get comfortable, let your eyes soften or close, and take a few deep breaths in and out.

Once you're settled, take some moments to choose someone who triggers a Part/reaction/response in you that you'd like to explore, understand better, or work with.

 As you picture this person, notice what it's like to be with them, how you feel, what you think, and how your body responds.

Now ask yourself, what do I imagine is this person's core belief about me or their core message to me? Write down what you believe their core beliefs/messages are.

Once you've identified what you imagine is their core belief or message, scan your body and find the first reaction/response/feeling you notice; you can notice this as how one Part of you reacts. Invite the Part to write below what it wants to say to or about the person who triggers you.

Recommended minimum write time: 3–5 minutes

_____

_____

_____

_____

_____

_____

_____

_____

_____

_____

_____

_____

_____

_____

_____

_____

_____

_____

_____

_____

_____

_____

_____

_____

_____

_____

_____

_____

INSTRUCTIONS

Re-read what the Part of you journaled. Now bring your awareness to the 8 C qualities we explored in Week 1 Exercise 1. If it's helpful, you can do the Exercise 1 Meditation here to reconnect with any of those qualities. Choose one of the qualities and write a response to the Part from that quality. Repeat this step so that you write a response from several of the qualities below.

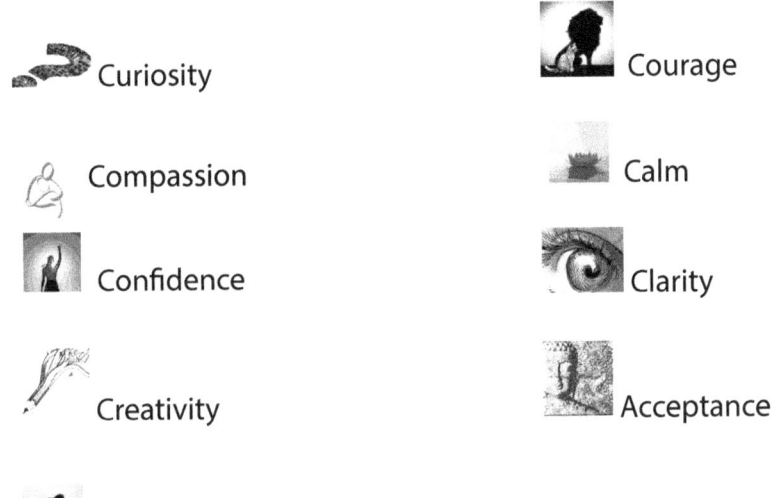

Curiosity

Compassion

Confidence

Creativity

Connection

Courage

Calm

Clarity

Acceptance

Recommended minimum write time: 3–5 minutes per quality

Write a response from _____

_____

_____

_____

_____

_____

_____

_____

_____

_____

Write a response from _____

_____

_____

_____

_____

_____

_____

_____

_____

_____

Write a response from _____

_____

_____

_____

_____

_____

_____

_____

_____

_____

OPTIONAL

Repeat the above sequence, starting again with the Meditation until all reacting parts have written and received feedback from Self qualities.

_____

_____

_____

_____

_____

_____

_____

_____

_____

_____

_____

_____

_____

_____

_____

_____

_____

REFLECTION WRITE

Re-read what you've journaled and write a reflection on the process of writing, any insights/awarenesses that came from journaling, or anything else you noticed.

Recommended minimum write time: 3 minutes

_____

_____

_____

_____

_____

_____

_____

_____

_____

_____

_____

_____

_____

_____

_____

_____

_____

_____

CONFIDENCE

When light fades at the end of day,
there is no loss of confidence.
Colors deepen in the gray, and
forms take the larger shape of their shadows
never losing authenticity. The waves
continue to wash to shore as
tides ebb and flow even on moonless
nights when we long for more, wrapped
in insecurities.

WEEK 5 – JOURNALING THE DAY: SELF-LED MOMENTS

EXERCISE 5

SUGGESTED TIME: 10–45 MINUTES

By now you should feel quite familiar with the qualities of Self and hopefully have a personal experience of what it's like to have access to your Self energy. As with most things, the more you practice accessing Self qualities and being in Self energy, the more it will become your natural state. Frequency and duration over time really count.

This exercise is designed to be an easy way for you to adopt a practice of bringing your awareness to Self and amplifying the experience. It's designed to be as long or as brief as you'd like so you can fit it into your daily routine and make it a habit. Spend as much or as little time as on this exercise as you want, but be sure to repeat it frequently. If you want to do it as a short daily practice, you can try spending 2 minutes on a couple of qualities each day, and 2 minutes on the REFLECTION WRITE. This will allow you to write for 10 minutes or less.

I do recommend, during Week 5 of this program, that you write about all 8 C qualities, Acceptance, and any others you've added. This will give you insight into noticing how all of them can add depth and value. You may think you won't find examples of all the qualities, but stay with it, open and curious; they almost always do come into awareness. If it helps to pull in examples from the week rather than just the day, that's a fine option too.

There are only 2 writing prompts for this exercise. The first will be a prompt to write about times during your day when you experienced the qualities of Self. The second prompt is the REFLECTION WRITE.

EXAMPLE

Below is an example from my own life when I was incredibly stressed due to moving households following a divorce. I used this exercise because I could do it quickly without needing to find a lot of quiet, alone time. The examples were readily available following a few deeper breaths. Doing this exercise during that time helped me feel less stressed, more grounded, and gave me perspective when I had extreme thoughts and fears. That perspective shift even allowed me to feel gratitude most of the time in spite of the crazy demands on me.

You can write about a topic or theme in your life as I did with my move or you can write about examples that aren't necessarily associated. For example, an incident of connection in the grocery store and a moment of calm over morning coffee and creativity at work. You'll see in my example where I wrote a little longer, even waxing poetic. Remember to always write in a way that channels what you want to say in the way that calls to you. There are no "shoulds" other than that.

Curiosity – Today I brought in curiosity when I toured and tried on the idea of living in the townhouse that we visited. Parts of me were discouraged and seeing the worst, but I stayed curious and open, trusting.

Compassion – Today compassion showed up when I saw L struggling with the idea of moving. My impatience with her softened and I could give her a hug.

Connection – Today I felt connection when the T-Mobile sales guy was kind and helpful after I told him about my stress. All the energy in my body softened.

Courage – Today it took courage to make the low counter offer for the sales commission to the buyer's agent in spite of part of me feeling shame and guilt. I was able to trust I wasn't doing anything wrong or hurtful and the offer was accepted.

WEEK 5

Gratitude – Today I felt so much gratitude when my phone wasn't really broken after I had asked the universe for some grace. All the bracing in my system relaxed.

Calm – Today I'm feeling lots of calm now as I write about and realize my gratitude. If I were to embody calm during this move, I wouldn't feel the anxiety that surges through my body or the stabbing seizing in my heart. My head would clear and my face would unfurrow. Deep breaths would come naturally.

Creativity – Today creativity showed up in my conversation with L as I talked to her about what would help her be okay with moving to a new place. It opened both of us to new possibilities and the strain between us fell away.

Confidence – Today I shifted into feeling confident when writing helped me be aware that I'll be okay even though this move buckles me in moments. Again my body relaxed and I felt more energetic to tackle everything that still needs to be done.

Clarity – Today I had a moment of clarity and asked L if we could be kind to each other during this terribly stressful time. I recognized that we were being reactive to one another because of our stress and asking this changed us from being at odds to wanting to support each other. If I brought clarity to these moving times, I would know that I'll weather the storm and land on the remote shore, dry, in one piece, with all my abilities. I'll see again a sun-drenched day when I can relax, breathe deeply, and smell my sun-warmed skin and hair as I lay washed up on the beach.

Acceptance – Today I moved into acceptance when I realized things may not go smoothly and may cost a lot of money or bring less money than I think I'll need, but I can accept and manage. This helped lots of parts of me feel less urgent and desperate to make things go a certain way.

INSTRUCTIONS

WEEK 5 Day 1: Bring your awareness to the 8 C qualities we've been exploring all week listed below. If it's helpful, you can do the Exercise 1 Meditation from Week 1 to reconnect with any of those qualities.

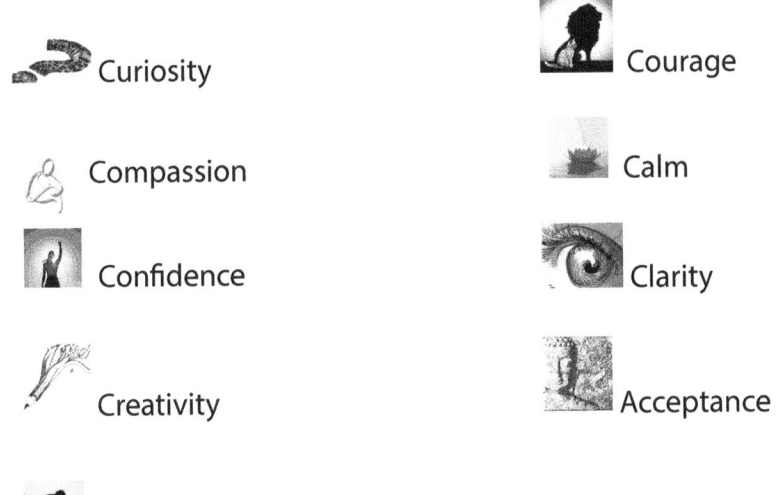

Curiosity

Courage

Compassion

Calm

Confidence

Clarity

Creativity

Acceptance

Connection

For each C quality of Self, write for a few minutes about times during the day when you felt or led with that quality. If nothing comes to mind for a quality, write about when you could have led from that quality.

MEDITATION

Get comfortable, let your eyes soften or close, and take a few deep breaths in and out.

Allow yourself to observe your breath and let your body settle from the day. Once you're settled take a last deep breath in and out and begin to write.

Recommended minimum write time: 2–5 minutes per quality

Write about when you had 🔍 Curiosity

_____

_____

_____

_____

_____

_____

_____

_____

_____

Write about when you had 🧘 Compassion

_____

_____

_____

_____

_____

_____

_____

_____

_____

Write about when you had Confidence

_____

_____

_____

_____

_____

_____

_____

_____

_____

Write about when you had Creativity

_____

_____

_____

_____

_____

_____

_____

_____

_____

Write about when you had Connection

_____

_____

_____

_____

_____

_____

_____

_____

Write about when you had Courage

_____

_____

_____

_____

_____

_____

_____

_____

Write about when you had Calm

_____

_____

_____

_____

_____

_____

_____

_____

_____

Write about when you had Clarity

_____

_____

_____

_____

_____

_____

_____

_____

_____

Write about when you had Acceptance

_____

_____

_____

_____

_____

_____

_____

_____

_____

REFLECTION WRITE

Re-read what you've journaled and write a reflection on the process of writing, any insights/awarenesses that came from journaling, or anything else you noticed.

Recommended minimum write time: 3 minutes

_____

_____

_____

_____

_____

_____

_____

_____

_____

_____

_____

_____

_____

_____

_____

_____

INSTRUCTIONS

WEEK 5 Day 2: Bring your awareness to the 8 C qualities we've been exploring all week listed below. If it's helpful, you can do the Exercise 1 Meditation from Week 1 to reconnect with any of those qualities.

Curiosity

Courage

Compassion

Calm

Confidence

Clarity

Creativity

Acceptance

Connection

For each C quality of Self, write for a few minutes about times during the day when you felt or led with that quality. If nothing comes to mind for a quality, write about when you could have led from that quality.

MEDITATION

Get comfortable, let your eyes soften or close, and take a few deep breaths in and out.

Allow yourself to observe your breath and let your body settle from the day. Once you're settled take a last deep breath in and out and begin to write.

Recommended minimum write time: 2–5 minutes per quality

Write about when you had Curiosity

_____

_____

_____

_____

_____

_____

_____

_____

_____

Write about when you had Compassion

_____

_____

_____

_____

_____

_____

_____

_____

_____

Write about when you had Confidence

_____

_____

_____

_____

_____

_____

_____

_____

_____

Write about when you had Creativity

_____

_____

_____

_____

_____

_____

_____

_____

_____

Write about when you had Connection

_____

_____

_____

_____

_____

_____

_____

_____

_____

Write about when you had Courage

_____

_____

_____

_____

_____

_____

_____

_____

_____

Write about when you had Calm

_____

_____

_____

_____

_____

_____

_____

_____

Write about when you had Clarity

_____

_____

_____

_____

_____

_____

_____

_____

_____

Write about when you had Acceptance

_____

_____

_____

_____

_____

_____

_____

_____

_____

REFLECTION WRITE

Re-read what you've journaled and write a reflection on the process of writing, any insights/awarenesses that came from journaling, or anything else you noticed.

Recommended minimum write time: 3 minutes

_____

_____

_____

_____

_____

_____

_____

_____

_____

_____

_____

_____

_____

_____

_____

_____

INSTRUCTIONS

WEEK 5 Day 3: Bring your awareness to the 8 C qualities we've been exploring all week listed below. If it's helpful, you can do the Exercise 1 Meditation from Week 1 to reconnect with any of those qualities.

Curiosity

Courage

Compassion

Calm

Confidence

Clarity

Creativity

Acceptance

Connection

For each C quality of Self, write for a few minutes about times during the day when you felt or led with that quality. If nothing comes to mind for a quality, write about when you could have led from that quality.

MEDITATION

Get comfortable, let your eyes soften or close, and take a few deep breaths in and out.

Allow yourself to observe your breath and let your body settle from the day. Once you're settled take a last deep breath in and out and begin to write.

Recommended minimum write time: 2–5 minutes per quality

Write about when you had Curiosity

_____

_____

_____

_____

_____

_____

_____

_____

_____

Write about when you had Compassion

_____

_____

_____

_____

_____

_____

_____

_____

_____

Write about when you had Confidence

_____

_____

_____

_____

_____

_____

_____

_____

_____

Write about when you had Creativity

_____

_____

_____

_____

_____

_____

_____

_____

_____

Write about when you had Connection

_____

_____

_____

_____

_____

_____

_____

_____

_____

Write about when you had Courage

_____

_____

_____

_____

_____

_____

_____

_____

_____

_____

Write about when you had Calm

_____

_____

_____

_____

_____

_____

_____

_____

_____

Write about when you had Clarity

_____

_____

_____

_____

_____

_____

_____

_____

_____

Write about when you had Acceptance

_____

_____

_____

_____

_____

_____

_____

_____

_____

REFLECTION WRITE

Re-read what you've journaled and write a reflection on the process of writing, any insights/awarenesses that came from journaling, or anything else you noticed.

Recommended minimum write time: 3 minutes

INSTRUCTIONS

WEEK 5 Day 4: Bring your awareness to the 8 C qualities we've been exploring all week listed below. If it's helpful, you can do the Exercise 1 Meditation from Week 1 to reconnect with any of those qualities.

Curiosity

Courage

Compassion

Calm

Confidence

Clarity

Creativity

Acceptance

Connection

For each C quality of Self, write for a few minutes about times during the day when you felt or led with that quality. If nothing comes to mind for a quality, write about when you could have led from that quality.

MEDITATION

Get comfortable, let your eyes soften or close, and take a few deep breaths in and out.

Allow yourself to observe your breath and let your body settle from the day. Once you're settled take a last deep breath in and out and begin to write.

Recommended minimum write time: 2–5 minutes per quality

Write about when you had ? Curiosity

_____

_____

_____

_____

_____

_____

_____

_____

_____

Write about when you had Compassion

_____

_____

_____

_____

_____

_____

_____

_____

_____

Write about when you had Confidence

_____

_____

_____

_____

_____

_____

_____

_____

Write about when you had Creativity

_____

_____

_____

_____

_____

_____

_____

_____

_____

Write about when you had Connection

_____

_____

_____

_____

_____

_____

_____

_____

_____

Write about when you had Courage

_____

_____

_____

_____

_____

_____

_____

_____

_____

Write about when you had Calm

_____

_____

_____

_____

_____

_____

_____

_____

_____

Write about when you had Clarity

_____

_____

_____

_____

_____

_____

_____

_____

_____

Write about when you had Acceptance

_____

_____

_____

_____

_____

_____

_____

_____

_____

_____

REFLECTION WRITE

Re-read what you've journaled and write a reflection on the process of writing, any insights/awarenesses that came from journaling, or anything else you noticed.

Recommended minimum write time: 3 minutes

_____

_____

_____

_____

_____

_____

_____

_____

_____

_____

_____

_____

_____

_____

_____

_____

INSTRUCTIONS

WEEK 5 Day 5: Bring your awareness to the 8 C qualities we've been exploring all week listed below. If it's helpful, you can do the Exercise 1 Meditation from Week 1 to reconnect with any of those qualities.

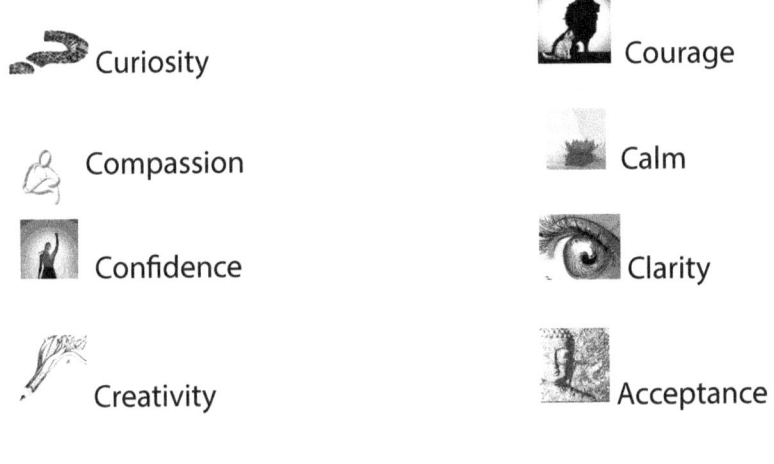

Curiosity

Courage

Compassion

Calm

Confidence

Clarity

Creativity

Acceptance

Connection

For each C quality of Self, write for a few minutes about times during the day when you felt or led with that quality. If nothing comes to mind for a quality, write about when you could have led from that quality.

MEDITATION

Get comfortable, let your eyes soften or close, and take a few deep breaths in and out.

Allow yourself to observe your breath and let your body settle from the day. Once you're settled take a last deep breath in and out and begin to write.

Recommended minimum write time: 2–5 minutes per quality

Write about when you had ➜ Curiosity

_____

_____

_____

_____

_____

_____

_____

_____

Write about when you had 🧘 Compassion

_____

_____

_____

_____

_____

_____

_____

_____

Write about when you had Confidence

_____

_____

_____

_____

_____

_____

_____

_____

_____

_____

Write about when you had Creativity

_____

_____

_____

_____

_____

_____

_____

_____

_____

_____

Write about when you had Connection

_____

_____

_____

_____

_____

_____

_____

_____

Write about when you had Courage

_____

_____

_____

_____

_____

_____

_____

_____

Write about when you had Calm

_____

_____

_____

_____

_____

_____

_____

_____

_____

Write about when you had Clarity

_____

_____

_____

_____

_____

_____

_____

_____

_____

Write about when you had Acceptance

_____

_____

_____

_____

_____

_____

_____

_____

_____

REFLECTION WRITE

Re-read what you've journaled and write a reflection on the process of writing, any insights/awarenesses that came from journaling, or anything else you noticed.

Recommended minimum write time: 3 minutes

_____

_____

_____

_____

_____

_____

_____

_____

_____

_____

_____

_____

_____

_____

_____

_____

_____

TAKING THE NEXT STEP

I dreamed I made my way to a place where
old barriers no longer confined me,
a place where old wounds no longer
defined me, a place where old fears
no longer consigned me.

When I looked down, I saw the path
to that place was at my feet
and so I took the next step, and then
the next, watching with curiosity.

WEEK 6 – REVIEW AND INTEGRATION

Hooray! You've made it to the final week of the program. Congratulations on the investment you've made in your wellness and wellbeing! This final week is an important one for anchoring everything you've done up till now so that you experience lasting benefits. Some of you won't want this program to end. For those of you who do, please don't cut corners now! Studies suggest the 6-week mark is where new habits are cemented.

This week there is no new exercise. Instead, you will use your writing days to review the 5 exercises you've already done during Weeks 1–5. For most of us, reviewing after a break is an important step in rooting content and experience for easy recall. It's also important for integration. Integration is the step where our experience is assimilated into the whole. From a systems perspective, it is critical for deep, lasting change.

Journal on!

INSTRUCTIONS

WEEK 6 Day 1: Choose one of the 8 C qualities of Self that you'd like to explore or have more of in your life:

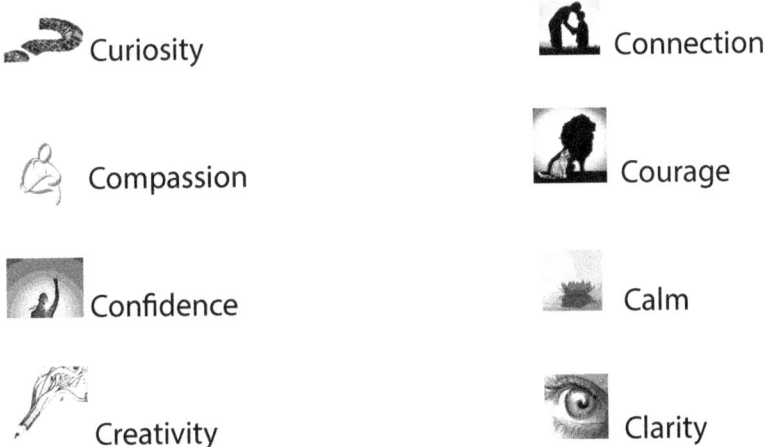

Curiosity

Connection

Compassion

Courage

Confidence

Calm

Creativity

Clarity

MEDITATION

Get comfortable, let your eyes soften or close, and take a few deep breaths in and out.

When you're settled, allow yourself to remember a time in your life when you had the quality you've chosen. If you don't remember having the quality, let yourself imagine what it might be like to have that quality. Just notice what you can. Take some time to remember or imagine what accompanies having this quality:

       the Physical Felt Sense,
            pause
       the Feelings,
            pause
       the Thinking and Thoughts,
            pause
       the Behaviors,
            pause
When you're ready, write about the experience of having this quality.

Recommended minimum write time: 3 minutes
Optimal write time: 5–7 minutes

_____

_____

_____

_____

_____

_____

_____

_____

_____

_____

_____

_____

_____

_____

_____

_____

_____

REFLECTION WRITE

Re-read what you've journaled and write a reflection on the process of writing about this quality, any insights/awarenesses that came from journaling, or anything else you noticed.

Recommended minimum write time: 3 minutes

_____

_____

_____

_____

_____

_____

_____

_____

_____

_____

_____

_____

_____

_____

_____

_____

_____

_____

OPTIONAL

Repeat the exercise to experience several or all of the C qualities of Self. Add the quality of Acceptance or any other quality you associate with being in Self energy to write about.

_____

_____

_____

_____

_____

_____

_____

_____

_____

_____

_____

_____

_____

_____

_____

_____

INSTRUCTIONS

WEEK 6 DAY 2: Choose a Part of yourself that you'd like to understand better, know more about, or work with. A Part may show up as a reaction, behavior, physical condition, body sensation, or strong feeling. When it's time to write about the Part, you have options:

- You can write in your own voice about this Part,
- You can allow this Part to write what it wants to say, or
- You can write for this Part saying what it has said to or shown you.
- I encourage you to experiment with writing from these different perspectives throughout the week.

MEDITATION

Get comfortable, let your eyes soften or close, and take a few deep breaths in and out.
When you're settled, bring your awareness to the Part of you you've chosen. Let yourself get curious about this Part and how it shows up:

> the Physical Felt Sense or Energy of it,
> > *pause*
> Its Feelings,
> > *pause*
> Its Thinking and Thoughts,
> > *pause*
> Its Behaviors,
> > *pause*

When you're ready, write about what you noticed. You have options about how to write:

- You can write in your own voice about this Part,
- You can allow this Part to write what it wants to say, or
- You can write for this Part saying what it has said or shown you.

Recommended minimum write time: 5–10 minutes

WEEK 6 DAY 2:

_____

_____

_____

_____

_____

_____

_____

_____

_____

_____

_____

_____

_____

_____

_____

_____

_____

_____

INSTRUCTIONS

Re-read what you've written.

Now bring your awareness to the 8 C qualities we explored last week in Exercise 1. If it's helpful, you can do the Exercise 1 Meditation here to reconnect with any of those qualities. When you're ready, write a response to the Part you're spending time with from one, some, or all of the 8 C qualities of Self, and from Acceptance.

Recommended minimum write time: 3–5 minutes per quality

Write a response from **Curiosity**

_____

_____

_____

_____

_____

_____

_____

_____

_____

Write a response from **Compassion**

_____

_____

_____

_____

_____

_____

_____

_____

Write a response from **Connection**

_____

_____

_____

_____

_____

_____

_____

_____

_____

Write a response from **Calm**

_____

_____

_____

_____

_____

_____

_____

_____

_____

Write a response from **Courage**

_____

_____

_____

_____

_____

_____

_____

_____

_____

Write a response from **Creativity**

_____

_____

_____

_____

_____

_____

_____

_____

Write a response from **Confidence**

_____

_____

_____

_____

_____

_____

_____

_____

_____

Write a response from **Clarity**

_____

_____

_____

_____

_____

_____

_____

_____

_____

Write a response from **Acceptance**

_____

_____

_____

_____

_____

_____

_____

_____

_____

REFLECTION WRITE

Re-read what you've journaled and write a reflection on the process of writing from these qualities, any insights/awarenesses that came from journaling, or anything else you noticed.

Recommended minimum write time: 3 minutes

_____

_____

_____

_____

_____

_____

_____

_____

_____

_____

_____

_____

_____

_____

_____

_____

INSTRUCTIONS

WEEK 6 Day 3: Take a few moments to think about and select a personal issue, problem, concern, or behavior that you'd like to understand more about.

Name what you've selected in the center circle of the Cluster Write template provided.

For each of the labeled boxes on the template, write 1–3 quick associations next to the box. Write as quickly as possible without judging or censoring what comes to mind. This helps you to access subconscious material.

Recommended minimum write time: 5–7 minutes

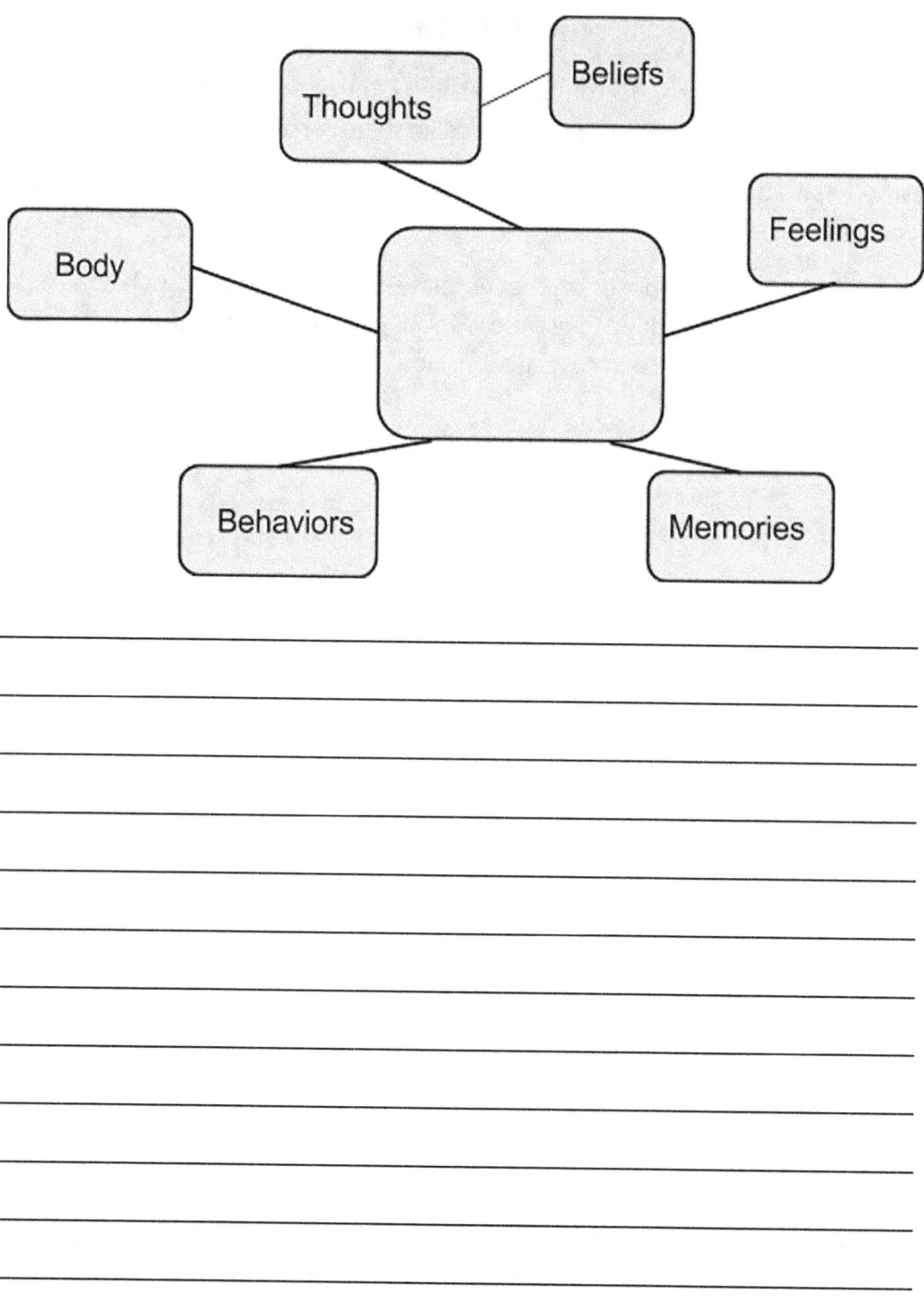

Beliefs

Thoughts

Feelings

Body

Behaviors

Memories

_____

_____

_____

_____

_____

_____

_____

_____

_____

_____

_____

Take a couple of moments to review your cluster. Notice within the cluster anything that feels like a Part of you and circle or label it. Typically, you'll see a number of Parts associated with the cluster. For example, if you started with Depression (one of your Parts) as your issue to explore (in the center box), you may find an Expectation Part who has a general fear and expectation of getting in trouble, a Behavior Part who acts out by drinking because of that fear, and a Memory Part who holds the memory of always being in trouble with your parents.

If you'd like to go the next step, you can use a solid line to connect Parts of you that are aligned and a squiggly line to connect Parts of you that are at odds. For instance, in the example above, there's the Feeling Part who drinks to manage fear and there might be a Feeling Part who has shame about that. These would be connected with a squiggly line. The Part with the expectation of getting in trouble would be connected with a solid line to the Part who drinks. Don't worry if your sheet gets messy.

Recommended minimum write time: 5 minutes

Now bring your awareness to the 8 C qualities we explored in Week 1 Exercise 1. If it's helpful, you can do the Exercise 1 Meditation here to reconnect with any of those qualities.

Choose one of the 8 C qualities of Self, the quality of Acceptance, or one of your own choosing. Write for a couple of minutes about what it is like or would be like to bring that quality to this cluster of Parts.

Then select another Self quality and write for a couple of minutes about what it is like or would be like to bring that quality to this cluster. Allow time so that you can explore a couple or all of the qualities below.

Recommended minimum write time: 5 minutes per quality

Curiosity

Courage

Compassion

Calm

Confidence

Clarity

Creativity

Acceptance

Connection

Write a response from _____

_____

_____

_____

_____

_____

_____

_____

_____

_____

Write a response from _____

_____

_____

_____

_____

_____

_____

_____

_____

_____

Write a response from _____

_____

_____

_____

_____

_____

_____

_____

_____

_____

REFLECTION WRITE

Re-read what you've journaled and write a reflection on the process of doing the cluster, identifying Parts, and writing from Self qualities, including any insights/awarenesses that came from journaling, or anything else you noticed.

Recommended minimum write time: 3 minutes

_____

_____

_____

_____

_____

_____

_____

_____

_____

_____

_____

_____

_____

_____

_____

_____

WEEK 6 Day 4:

MEDITATION

Get comfortable, let your eyes soften or close, and take a few deep breaths in and out.

Once you're settled, take some moments to choose someone who triggers a Part/reaction/response in you that you'd like to explore, understand better, or work with.

 As you picture this person, notice what it's like to be with them, how you feel, what you think, and how your body responds.

Now ask yourself, what do I imagine is this person's core belief about me or their core message to me? Write down what you believe their core beliefs/messages are.

Once you've identified what you imagine is their core belief or message, scan your body and find the first reaction/response/feeling you notice; you can notice this as how one Part of you reacts. Invite the Part to write below what it wants to say to or about the person who triggers you.

Recommended minimum write time: 3–5 minutes

_____

_____

_____

_____

_____

_____

_____

_____

INSTRUCTIONS

Re-read what the Part of you journaled. Now bring your awareness to the 8 C qualities we explored in Week 1 Exercise 1. If it's helpful, you can do the Exercise 1 Meditation here to reconnect with any of those qualities. Choose one of the qualities and write a response to the Part from that quality. Repeat this step so that you write a response from several of the qualities below.

Curiosity

Courage

Compassion

Calm

Confidence

Clarity

Creativity

Acceptance

Connection

Recommended minimum write time: 3–5 minutes per quality

Write a response from _____

_____

_____

_____

_____

_____

_____

_____

_____

Write a response from _____

_____

_____

_____

_____

_____

_____

_____

_____

Write a response from _____

_____

_____

_____

_____

_____

_____

_____

_____

_____

OPTIONAL

Repeat the above sequence, starting again with the Meditation until all reacting parts have written and received feedback from Self qualities.

_____

_____

_____

_____

_____

_____

_____

_____

_____

_____

_____

_____

_____

_____

_____

_____

_____

_____

_____

_____

REFLECTION WRITE

Re-read what you've journaled and write a reflection on the process of writing, any insights/awarenesses that came from journaling, or anything else you noticed.

Recommended minimum write time: 3 minutes

_____

_____

_____

_____

_____

_____

_____

_____

_____

_____

_____

_____

_____

_____

_____

_____

_____

_____

_____

INSTRUCTIONS

WEEK 6 Day 5: Bring your awareness to the 8 C qualities we've been exploring all week listed below. If it's helpful, you can do the Exercise 1 Meditation from Week 1 to reconnect with any of those qualities.

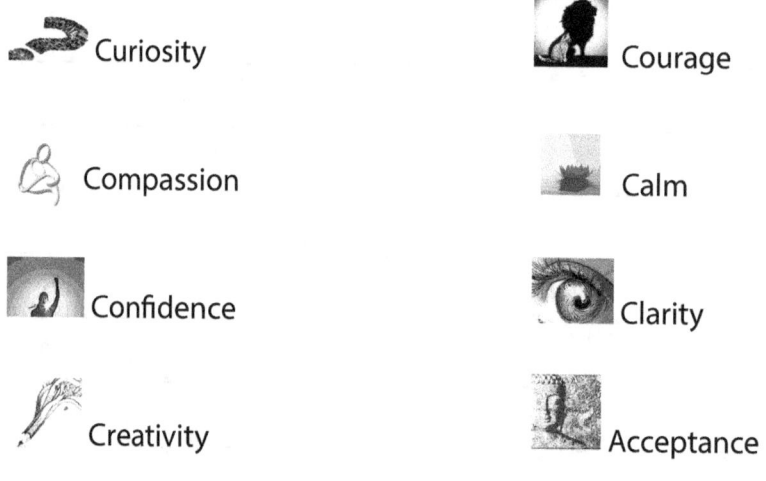

Curiosity

Courage

Compassion

Calm

Confidence

Clarity

Creativity

Acceptance

 Connection

For each C quality of Self, write for a few minutes about times during the day when you felt or led with that quality. If nothing comes to mind for a quality, write about when you could have led from that quality.

MEDITATION

Get comfortable, let your eyes soften or close, and take a few deep breaths in and out.

Allow yourself to observe your breath and let your body settle from the day. Once you're settled take a last deep breath in and out and begin to write.

Recommended minimum write time: 2–5 minutes per quality

Write about when you had Curiosity

_____

_____

_____

_____

_____

_____

_____

_____

_____

Write about when you had Compassion

_____

_____

_____

_____

_____

_____

_____

_____

_____

Write about when you had Confidence

_____

_____

_____

_____

_____

_____

_____

_____

_____

Write about when you had Creativity

_____

_____

_____

_____

_____

_____

_____

_____

_____

Write about when you had Connection

_____

_____

_____

_____

_____

_____

_____

_____

_____

Write about when you had Courage

_____

_____

_____

_____

_____

_____

_____

_____

_____

Write about when you had Calm

_____

_____

_____

_____

_____

_____

_____

_____

_____

Write about when you had Clarity

_____

_____

_____

_____

_____

_____

_____

_____

_____

Write about when you had Acceptance

_____

_____

_____

_____

_____

_____

_____

_____

_____

_____

REFLECTION WRITE

Re-read what you've journaled and write a reflection on the process of writing, any insights/awarenesses that came from journaling, or anything else you noticed.

Recommended minimum write time: 3 minutes

_____

_____

_____

_____

_____

_____

_____

_____

_____

_____

_____

_____

_____

_____

_____

_____

_____

CLOSING

Some things to consider now that you've completed this program:

Writing is intentional, focused, not multitasking—features all shared with mindfulness. Congratulations to you on learning a new mindfulness practice!

Dr. James Pennebaker has spent his career researching the therapeutic benefits of writing (1986). Some of his findings include:

- Writing lowers stress responses and emotional reactivity through allowing us to name, make meaning, and come to terms with experiences; through slowing our mind down to organize thinking about an event or experience.

- Writing produces brain changes, including changes to brain process and thinking. With negative experiences or events, our brain will keep obsessing if we don't figure out cause and prevention.

- Writing improves sleep, which allows healing, enhances immune function, and improves general functioning and cognitive processing.

- Writing that reduces stress and emotional activation, resulting in healthy changes such as improved working memory, social connections, general life functioning, and physical health.

- Writing about positive experiences results in the same or better health benefits as writing about negative experiences.

- You might reflect on these outcomes to see whether you're experiencing any of the benefits. Sometimes our baseline changes gradually over time and we fail to notice!

Neuroplasticity allows for changes to our brain and nervous system. What we focus on, pay attention to, practice (repetition), and spend time on (duration) is what we reinforce. "What fires together, wires together."

CLOSING

Are you noticing being in Self energy and having access to Self qualities more of the time thanks to your practice with this program over the past weeks?

The brain is "velcro" for negative and threatening things. It is evolutionarily adaptive for us to pay attention to what can hurt us. This leads to states like anxiety, depression, pessimism, and shame, all of which can be seen as threat response states with underlying fight, flight, freeze, or shame protective responses.

Are you noticing being in threat responses less often as a result of supporting the Parts of you that may be in those states with Self energy?

The brain is "teflon" for positive and joyful things. Evolutionarily, there's no advantage to having these times deeply engraved in our awareness. Positive experiences enhance our lives but are not essential for survival. We have to be intentional to adopt and integrate these states.

Are you noticing being in positive and joyful states more often? Do they feel more integrated?

RESOURCES and REFERENCES

www.ifs-institute.com IFS Institute website.

https://journaltherapy.com/ The Center for Journal Therapy website.

https://www.amazon.com/stores/page/F7818742-54B0-4A8F-8DED-F5CFFC3B2148. Center for Journal Therapy Amazon store.

Adams, Kathleen. 2006. Journal therap: Writing as a therapeutic tool: A training workbook. Brentwood, TN: Cross Country Education.

Adams, Kathleen. 2013. Expressive Writing: Foundations of Practice. Rowman and Littlefield Education. Lanham, MD.

Baikie, Karen A., and Wilhelm, Karen. 2018. Emotional and Physical Health Benefits of Expressive Writing. Published online by Cambridge University Press

ACKNOWLEDGEMENTS

Exercise 4 is adapted from a handout from Michi Rose, one of the original Lead IFS Trainers.

The exercises are informed by the work and writing of Kay Adams, the author of Journal to the Self and founder of The Therapeutic Writing Institute and The Center for Journal Therapy – www.journaltherapy.com

Heather Leavesley, MA, MA, IFSCP, is in private practice and owns InnerLight Coaching and Psychotherapy in Centennial, CO. She is a Certified IFS Practitioner and has been a Certified Journal Trainer for Kay Adam's Journal to the Self. Heather offers workshops throughout the year and works with clients at her office and via online virtual sessions.

You can learn more about her services and products at www.hlcounseling.com.

www.ingramcontent.com/pod-product-compliance
Lightning Source LLC
Chambersburg PA
CBHW080839120626
46553CB00009B/2499